FOOD FOR SHARING

FOOD FOR SHARING

Love and Spices from an Immigrant Kitchen

Ashia Ismail-Singer
Photography by Lottie Hedley

Interlink Books

an imprint of Interlink Publishing Group, Inc.
Northampton, Massachusetts

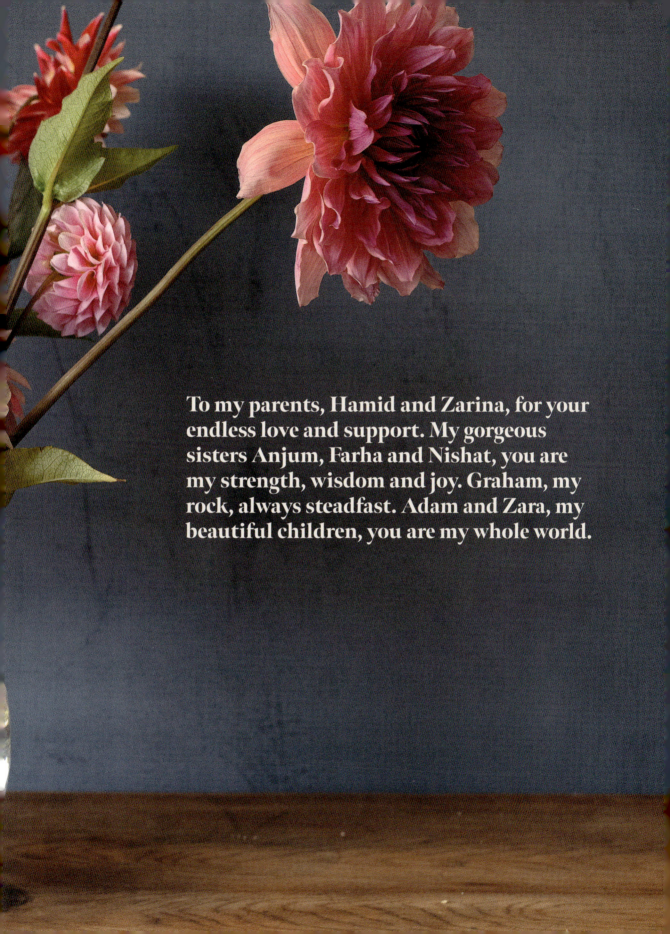

To my parents, Hamid and Zarina, for your endless love and support. My gorgeous sisters Anjum, Farha and Nishat, you are my strength, wisdom and joy. Graham, my rock, always steadfast. Adam and Zara, my beautiful children, you are my whole world.

Introduction	09
Breakfast & brunch	17
Summer picnics & alfresco dining	49
Glorious vegetables	81
Elaborate dinners & festive feasts	115
Sunset snacks & sharing plates	147
Sugar & spice	183
Menus	227
Extras	241
With thanks	247
Index	251

Contents

I simply cannot believe that I am sitting here writing my introduction for this book. It is the culmination of my love of food, cooking and entertaining. I have created the recipes in this book to be as simple as possible, inspired by the spices I grew up with. When it comes to spices, their endless culinary possibilities make my soul sing. Every element of this book is a fusion of flavors and cultures, overflowing with the joy of sharing food, gathered together with loved ones. From India to Africa, the Middle East, France, the UK and New Zealand, this book will take you on a journey full of flavor with dishes from the melded cultures that make up my extended family.

Introduction

My home-cooked dishes are simple yet packed with flavor, using fresh ingredients and some key spices that blend cultures and traditions. Mine is an immigrant's cuisine, of sorts, merging old traditions with new ones, creating food that spans generations, geography and ethnicities. This is my story.

Food evokes a passion in me that I cherish, one that has grown from my early childhood days in Malawi, Africa, to my teenage years in England, and the last twenty-plus years in my beautiful, adopted home country of New Zealand.

Being of Indian heritage, my love of cooking first started at an early age, and some of my favorite recipes are ones that have been passed down through my family, adapted by each generation to suit the ingredients available. As someone who wears many hats, I cook and create recipes, source props and style. As well as this, I have a "day job" as a nurse and I have just retrained to start a career in real estate, with the hope of making real estate and food writing my full-time gigs.

My grandparents were Memon Muslims who came from Gujarat, on the western coast of India. Sometime in the late 1930s to early 1940s, they emigrated to Malawi, Africa. Memons originated in the northwestern part of ancient India, the Sindh region of modern-day Pakistan. The Memon language has similar vocabulary to the Sindhi, Kutchi and Gujarati languages, and also shares cultural similarities with the Khoja, Khatri and Gujarati people. Memon lineage traces back to Lohanas of Sindh, and the origin of the name Memon comes from the word *mumin*, or "believer" in Arabic. The Memon community was founded in the fifteenth century when they converted to Islam.

Memons were predominantly merchant traders of the Sunni Muslim sect. They were very business-minded and philanthropic, making sure that their community was well looked after. Due to their mercantile nature, they were never afraid to migrate and progress. Migration led Memons to Africa, to Asia, to the Americas and to the Middle East. My grandparents left India to migrate to Africa, first to Mozambique, and then to Malawi, to build a business and advance themselves.

My dad was born in India, in Jamnagar, in the southwestern part of Gujarat. He was only one year old when his family left for Malawi, known as the "warm heart of Africa." My mother's family were already in Malawi, and she was born there. My sisters and I were all also born in Malawi. Because of political instability, we left as a family in 1987 to immigrate to England. We all had British passports, as Malawi is part of the Commonwealth, and my father had lived and studied in the UK during the 1960s. It was a chance for a better life for us all.

Regardless of where we lived, cooking was always a big part of our upbringing. My parents loved to entertain, and my mom had no qualms about cooking a biryani, a layered meat and rice dish,

Top left: Celebrating my sister Nishat's first birthday in our home in Malawi. (L to R) Farha, me, Mom (Zarina), Nishat and Anjum. **Top right:** Celebrating Nishat's second birthday. (L to R) Mom, me, Nishat, Anjum and Farha. **Second row left:** My dad, Hamid, with me and Anjum walking up Capital Hill, a favorite pastime of ours at that age. **Second row middle:** Anjum and me at a school fair. **Second row right:** Anjum and me all dressed up on our way to a friend's birthday party. **Third row left:** Me and Anjum in matching bathing suits at a friend's beach house in Salima, Malawi. **Third row right:** Me and Anjum looking out at Lake Malawi in Mangochi. Our family used to often go to the lake for the school vacations when we were growing up. **Bottom row left:** Me and my sister Anjum celebrating our sixteenth birthday at our home in Lilongwe, Malawi. **Bottom row right:** Me and my sister Anjum celebrating our eighteenth birthday in Coventry, after we had moved as a family to the United Kingdom.

INTRODUCTION

> **"I remember the fragrant smells of spices cooking, beautifully aromatic, heady, a mixture of hot, salty, sweet and sour, perfectly balanced."**

for a hundred guests on special occasions. Together, my mom and dad always planned what dishes were to be served at family gatherings.

We celebrated every festival and special family occasion with an abundance of food. My parents loved having parties for our birthdays, especially since my sister and I are twins. There weren't very many twins in our social circle, so we were a bit of a novelty! Religious festivities, like Eid, were always spent with wider family and friends, and there would be meat and vegetarian dishes, my mom's famous biryani (the recipe for which is on page 123) and, of course, lots of amazing sweets and desserts.

I loved being in the kitchen with my mom, and with my aunts who would visit. Families always had an open-door policy, so you never needed an invite. Our cook, Medson, prepared the ingredients, and then Mom would come in and finish things off. He would make excellent rotis; my mom taught him, too. I remember the fragrant smells of spices cooking, beautifully aromatic, heady, a mixture of hot, salty, sweet and sour, perfectly balanced. Recipes were never written down but remembered by taking part, helping and learning as you went, developing your tastebuds, which became more attuned with age and experience. And this led to cooking by instinct, which is how I cook now.

In Malawi when I was growing up, fruit, vegetables and meat did not come packaged. We grew our produce or slaughtered the animals ourselves. We had a chicken coop, which also housed goats. A couple of times a week before heading off to work, my dad would slaughter a chicken by slitting its throat and saying a prayer, making it halal. Then our cook would pluck and clean the chicken before it was presented as dinner. Goats were slaughtered the same way, but only every couple of months, and the meat was prepared and then frozen for later use. This was our normal, and the way of life for me growing up in Africa. I have fond memories of going to the dairy farm with my sisters, my cousin, my mom and aunt to collect our milk, which we would carry home, sloshing about in a big aluminum milk pail. The ingredients we used were always fresh, and the dishes were predominantly Indian. But Mom was making "fusion food" long before fusion was fashionable. A confident cook, she effortlessly adapted Western recipes—Sunday roasts, casseroles and shepherd's pie—to incorporate Indian flavors.

Moving to the UK from Malawi was an eye-opening journey. Although my father had lived in the UK in the 1960s, things had changed a lot when we immigrated there as a family in 1987. Before we immigrated, we had traveled as a family to the UK several times on vacation. But moving there as a teenager was a culture shock, having lived a very different lifestyle with open spaces, big yards and fruit trees, to then come to a country where you could see into your neighbor's backyard from the windows on the second floor. It was also quite confronting, coming across people who didn't accept you because you were different.

I navigated this new life with apprehension. But what brought me comfort and joy was being part of a close-knit family and coming home from college and cooking dinner. Both my parents

> **"We all need food to sustain us. It nourishes life. It makes us who we are and creates memories that link us to our families and friends."**

worked, and my sister and I, being the eldest of four girls, would come home and start cooking the family meal. I was studying fashion and design at art school, and I loved getting creative in the kitchen, too. It was here that my love of cooking blossomed. There was a large population of South Asians in the UK, and we could go to the Indian grocery stores and get spices and vegetables that we were used to. But we also started using ingredients that we hadn't been able to get in Malawi and so the melding of food cultures continued, creating recipes that built bridges between all the countries I have called home.

Moving countries on my own in 1997 was probably the most exciting—and also the hardest—thing I ever did. Always outspoken, adventurous and passionate, I followed my wanderlust. I eventually arrived in New Zealand, falling in love not just with the country but with one Kiwi in particular, who I ended up marrying and having two amazing children with. Now, having spent more of my life in New Zealand than anywhere else, I truly call it home. But that doesn't stop me from being an immigrant and missing "home," which is ultimately wherever the rest of my family is.

This book includes some treasured recipes my mom taught me. And it's full of recipes I have created, trying to recapture the flavors of my childhood. There are Indian, British and Kiwi dishes, and also some Middle Eastern and French dishes inspired by my two sisters who married French Algerians. Our family celebrations are always a mix of recipes from these cultures, and nothing brings me more joy than to share them with you.

This book is a beautiful, flavorful journey. In the Breakfast & Brunch and Summer Picnics & Alfresco Dining chapters, the recipes are created for the way we live today. Eating fresh, seasonal ingredients without compromising flavor. There's a whole chapter of Glorious Vegetables to inspire you to eat more greens, and Sunset Snacks & Sharing Plates for party inspiration. Elaborate Dinners & Festive Feasts will cover all your momentous occasions, from birthdays and anniversaries to religious festivities. And the icing on the cake is Sugar & Spice and all things nice—desserts with a hint of spice, a perfect ending to this delectable journey of sharing, connecting and making memories with those you love. Towards the end of the book there are menu ideas for dinner parties. Be inspired by them, use them as they are, or tweak them to make them your own. Take a picture of the menu card and use it as an invitation for your guests, they will love it!

Every family—every person—has a story. Where they come from and where they end up is circumstantial. But, along the way, we all need food to sustain us. It nourishes our lives. It makes us who we are and creates memories that link us to our families and friends.

I have relished every minute of this amazing journey, and I'm delighted to be sharing these recipes with you. I believe that food celebrates life. So, I hope that my food feeds your imagination to cook fabulous meals to share with your family and friends, ones that help create wonderful memories with those you cherish.

Much love,
Ashia

Breakfast for me is usually a cup of tea. I am not a morning person—I get up at the very last minute, after having snoozed the alarm a dozen times! But my husband and children wake up hungry. So, quick, easy breakfasts are key—usually oats, cereals and eggs. I prefer a slower start, especially on the weekends. These recipes are perfect for those leisurely weekends where you invite friends and family around to share a lazy breakfast with. From spiced lamb shakshuka to cinnamon and cardamom doughnuts, there is something in this chapter for everyone.

Breakfast & brunch

Kathi rolls with pickled onion & lamb kebab

Makes 6

for the pickled onions
1 cup (240 ml) water
1 cup (240 ml) white wine vinegar or white vinegar
1 tbsp salt
¼ cup (50 g) sugar
2 red onions, thinly sliced (a mandolin works well)
2 green chiles, thinly sliced (optional)
1½ tsp black or pink peppercorns

for the kebabs
handful of fresh cilantro
1–2 green chiles
2 lb 4 oz (1 kg) ground lamb
2–3 garlic cloves, crushed
1 onion, peeled and finely chopped
1 heaped tsp ground cumin
1 heaped tsp ground coriander
1 heaped tsp ground turmeric
1 egg
salt and ground black pepper
2 tbsp olive oil, for frying

for the kathi rolls
6 parathas (see page 241)
6 free-range eggs
salt and ground black pepper
handful of chopped fresh cilantro, plus extra to serve
2–3 tbsp oil, for frying

to serve
cilantro, torn
cilantro chutney (see page 152)

Growing up we didn't have sandwiches in our lunchboxes, we had roti rolls, sometimes with leftover daal or omelet or a dry potato curry. This recipe is next level—homemade paratha (see page 241) with a layer of omelet and kebabs, topped with pickled onions and chutney. You can cook the kebabs in a frying pan or on the grill, or, you could use chargrilled pieces of chicken or lamb.

For the pickled onions: Heat the water, vinegar, salt and sugar in a saucepan over medium heat, until the salt and sugar have dissolved. Set aside to cool. In a 1 pint (500 ml) jar, combine the onions, chiles and peppercorns. Add the vinegar mixture to the jar. Allow to cool before sealing. Once the pickled onions are tender and bright pink they are ready to use. They will keep in the fridge for a week or so.

For the kebabs: In a blender, blend the cilantro and green chiles into a chunky paste.

In a large bowl, mix the ground lamb with all the other ingredients, including the cilantro-chile paste. The egg will bind it together, however, if the mixture is a little too wet, add some breadcrumbs.

To check the seasoning, take a small amount of mixture and fry in a pan until cooked. Taste and adjust seasoning, if necessary.

Divide the lamb mixture into about 20 even-sized balls, then mold them into long sausage shapes. A great trick my mom taught me, which also makes the kebabs cook through well, is to use a wooden spoon, molding each ball around the handle, so each is 3–4 in (8–10 cm) long (they will shrink when cooked). Gently slide the kebab off the handle and place on a tray.

When you are ready to cook, heat olive oil in a frying pan or griddle pan (if you are using a stovetop griddle pan you will not need much oil). Fry the kebabs over low–medium heat until nicely browned and cooked through, 10–12 minutes. You can also cook them on the grill—mold the meat around a wooden spoon then slide the kebab off and insert a metal skewer to help turn them during cooking on the grill.

Recipe continued overleaf . . .

For the kathi rolls: **Preheat the oven to 200°F (100°C). Place parathas in oven to keep warm for assembling.**

Lightly beat the eggs with salt, pepper and cilantro. Heat a frying pan over medium heat, add a teaspoon of oil, add your paratha and cook for 30 seconds. Next, add a sixth of the egg mixture on top of the paratha and spread it around. Flip the paratha and cook until the egg is set (I like mine a lovely light golden), flip again to brown the other side.

Repeat with remaining egg and parathas—you can keep these warm in the oven while you finish the rest.

To serve: Place the paratha on a plate, egg-side up. Cut the kebabs into bite-sized chunks and arrange down the middle, scatter with pickled onions and chopped cilantro, roll up and serve with cilantro chutney.

Tip You can make this vegetarian with mushrooms, cauliflower or potatoes, or chunks of paneer or haloumi, cooked to your liking. You don't have to reserve this recipe for brunch, you can enjoy it anytime of the day.

Vegetarian samosa chaat

Makes 20–24

for the samosa pastry
4 cups (500 g) all-purpose flour
1 tsp salt
1 tsp cumin seeds or carom seeds (optional)
scant ½ cup (100 ml) neutral oil
1–1¼ cups (280–300 ml) warm water

for the filling
1 lb 5 oz (600 g) starchy potatoes
1 tbsp olive oil
2 tsp mustard seeds
1 tsp salt
2–3 green chiles, finely chopped
1 tsp ground turmeric
1 tsp amchur (mango powder)
1 tsp ground coriander
1 tsp ground cumin
ground black pepper
1–2 tbsp finely chopped fresh cilantro
¾ cup (100 g) frozen peas
neutral oil, for deep-frying

for the flour paste
1 tbsp all-purpose flour
1 tbsp water

Ingredients continued overleaf . . .

A chaat is a savory Indian snack traditionally sold by street vendors. It has a base of samosas, potatoes or chickpeas and lots of different toppings, like crispy puri, chutneys, deep-fried noodles and yogurt. This dish takes time but it's so worth the effort. Great for brunch with family and friends.

For the pastry: Place the flour in a large bowl and mix in the salt and whole spices (if using). Make a well and pour in the oil. Slowly rub the oil into the flour until it resembles breadcrumbs. Add most of the water and bring together into a dough—you may not need to use all the water. Knead the dough until smooth, about 6–8 minutes, and leave to rest for 20–30 minutes, while you make the filling.

For the filling: Boil the potatoes (with skin on) in salty water until tender. Drain and cool then peel and roughly mash. Set aside.

Heat the oil in a large pot, add the mustard seeds and, once they start popping, add the salt, green chiles, then the spices, chopped cilantro, peas and mashed potatoes. Stir to combine, cook for a few minutes. Transfer to a platter and cool completely.

Once the dough has rested, divide it into 10–12 balls (each ball will make 2 samosas), depending on how large you want each samosa. Cover the balls with a damp cloth. Roll each ball into a 5½ x 7 in (14 cm x 18 cm) oval. Cut each oval in half crosswise.

Prepare a glue-like paste of the flour and water to seal the samosas. With the round edge of the dough facing towards you, fold both corners towards the middle, overlapping them by ¾–1 in (2–3 cm). Join the edges with the flour paste, making a cone shape, and leave a rounded top flap of 1–1½ in (3–4 cm). Fill each samosa with 1–2 tablespoons of filling then fold the flap over, sealing it with the flour paste.

Once all the samosas are filled, pour oil into a deep wok or pot so it comes halfway up the side. Place over medium heat. To check if the oil is hot enough, add a small piece of bread—if it turns golden, the oil is ready. (Be careful not to overheat the oil or the samosas will turn dark brown quickly and the insides won't be cooked.)

Recipe continued overleaf . . .

for the cilantro garlic chutney
bunch of fresh cilantro, about 2 oz (60 g)
1–2 green chiles
2 tbsp lemon or lime juice
small handful of fresh mint leaves
salt and ground black pepper
½–1 tsp sugar
½ tsp ground cumin
1 garlic clove, crushed
½–1 tbsp yogurt (optional)

for the chaat
⅔ cup (150 g) plain yogurt
2–3 tbsp cilantro garlic chutney (see above)
2–3 tbsp tamarind chutney (see page 242) or chile sauce
1 small red onion, finely diced
1 fresh tomato, finely diced
2–3 tbsp pomegranate seeds (optional)
2–3 tbsp sev (crunchy Indian noodles)
2 tbsp chopped fresh cilantro

Cook the samosas in batches until golden and crispy, 3–5 minutes on each side, making sure the oil is not too hot. Drain on paper towels.

For the cilantro garlic chutney: Using a food processor or blender, blend all the ingredients into a thick paste. You can add the yogurt to make it slightly creamier if you wish.

Arrange the samosas on a large platter, drizzle with yogurt and chutneys, top with diced onion, tomato, pomegranate seeds (if using), sev and cilantro. Dig in—it's the most amazing flavor bomb and will send your taste buds into a frenzy.

Tip You can buy amchur, sev, carom seeds and various chutneys from Indian food stores. Samosas can be prepared ahead of time and frozen. Just remove from the freezer 20 minutes before you want to fry them. Cilantro garlic chutney makes about ¾ cup (180 ml) and any leftovers can also be frozen.

Herby ciabatta with ricotta & cherries

Serves 4–6

1 lb 2 oz (500 g) pitted cherries (fresh or from a jar)
juice of 1 lemon
2 tbsp sugar
1 tbsp water
1 tsp cinnamon
2 tsp cornstarch
scant 1 cup (200 g) ricotta
3–4 tbsp olive oil
handful of finely chopped fresh herbs (basil, thyme, mint, cilantro)
1 loaf ciabatta bread, sliced
handful of chopped pistachios
honey, for drizzling
fresh herbs, to garnish

A great seasonal treat with sweet, ripe cherries and creamy ricotta that is equally delicious with pitted cherries out of a jar. The combination of the sweet cherries and honey and the slightly tangy ricotta goes perfectly with toasted bread.

Simmer the pitted cherries, juice of ½ lemon, sugar, water and cinnamon in a pot for 12–15 minutes. Mix some of the cherry juice from the jar, or water if using fresh cherries, with the cornstarch and add this to the pot to thicken the cherry sauce. Remove from the heat and set aside to cool.

In a small bowl, whisk the ricotta with the remaining lemon juice.

In a separate small bowl, combine the oil and chopped herbs, then brush this onto both sides of the sliced ciabatta. Heat a nonstick frying pan or griddle and toast the ciabatta slices on both sides.

Spread each slice of ciabatta with the ricotta mixture, top with cherries and their sauce, and finish with chopped pistachios, a drizzle of honey and herb sprigs.

Tip You can prepare the cherry topping and ricotta ahead of time. Brush and toast the ciabatta just before serving.

Cinnamon & cardamom breakfast doughnuts with blueberry compote

Makes 18

for the blueberry compote
2 cups (160 g) fresh or frozen blueberries
¼ cup (60 ml) maple syrup
2 tbsp water
juice of ½ lemon
½ tsp vanilla extract

for the doughnut balls
2 cups (240 g) all-purpose flour
⅓ cup (70 g) sugar, plus 3 tbsp
1 tbsp baking powder
1 tsp salt
5 tbsp (70 g) ice-cold butter
¾ cup (180 ml) milk
1 tsp ground cinnamon
1 tsp ground cardamom
neutral oil, for deep-frying
mascarpone or whipped cream, to serve

Who doesn't love doughnuts? These yeast-free doughnuts are perfect for brunch after you have had your savory meal. They are easy to make and paired with a berry compote are such a delight to eat. You can make the compote with any berries, fresh or frozen.

For the berry compote: In a small pot, combine half of the blueberries with the maple syrup, water, lemon juice and vanilla and simmer over medium heat for 8–10 minutes. Add the remaining blueberries and cook for a further 8–10 minutes, stirring occasionally. Remove from the heat and set aside to cool. The compote will thicken as it cools.

For the doughnuts: In a large bowl, whisk the flour, 3 tablespoons sugar, baking powder and salt until mixed. Grate the cold butter into the mix, add the milk and knead into a soft ball. Add a little more flour if it seems too sticky. Portion into 18 small balls, and roll until smooth. Place on a tray lined with parchment paper.

In a small bowl, combine the remaining sugar and the spices and set aside.

Pour oil into a large wok or pot so it comes a third of the way up the side. Place over medium–high heat. To check if the oil is hot enough, add a small piece of bread—if it turns golden, the oil is ready. Fry the doughnuts in batches, turning until golden and cooked through, approximately 1½ minutes. Drain on paper towels.

Toss the doughnuts in the cinnamon and cardamom sugar while still warm.

Serve with blueberry compote and mascarpone or whipped cream.

Tip You can easily double the recipe to serve more people. To get the butter ice cold, place in the freezer for 30 minutes.

Watermelon, feta & maple salad

Serves 4–6

1 red onion, sliced
juice of 1 lime
salt and ground black pepper
2 lb 4 oz (1 kg) watermelon, cubed
1 large cucumber, sliced into semi-circles
7 oz (200 g) feta, cubed
handful each of fresh mint and cilantro leaves, chopped, plus a few sprigs of mint to serve

for the maple dressing
juice of 1 lime
2 tbsp olive oil
drizzle of maple syrup
salt and ground black pepper
¼ tsp chile flakes (optional)

A gorgeous, easy salad with sweet and salty flavors and a little chile kick to liven everything up. Best eaten the day it's made. It's perfect as a side to any dish or on its own as a quick brunch on the run in summer.

Place the sliced red onion in a bowl and add lime juice and salt and pepper. Set aside.

Put the watermelon in a large serving dish and gently toss in the cucumber, feta and herbs.

For the maple syrup dressing: In a small jar, combine the lime juice, olive oil, maple syrup, salt and pepper, and chile flakes (if using)—I like the chile as it gives a subtle kick and works well with the sweetness of the maple. Put the lid on and give it a good shake.

Drain the onion and place on top of the salad. Drizzle with the dressing and toss. Garnish with mint sprigs and serve immediately.

Spiced lamb shakshuka

Serves 4–6

1 tbsp oil
1 medium onion, finely sliced
2–3 garlic cloves, crushed
1 tsp salt
1 lb 2 oz (500 g) ground lamb
14 oz (400 g) can diced tomato
1 tbsp tomato paste
1 tsp chile powder
1 tsp ground paprika
1 tsp ground coriander
½ tsp ground cumin
¼ tsp ground turmeric
½ tsp rose harissa or harissa
2 small potatoes (7 oz/200 g in total), diced
½ cup (70 g) frozen peas
4–6 eggs
handful of chopped fresh cilantro
kesra bread (see page 170) or naan (see page 241), to serve

Originally from North Africa, shakshuka is essentially a vegetarian dish, but I have given it a twist by using lamb. Growing up we often had ground lamb or beef curry with potatoes and peas served with fried eggs and roti for the perfect Sunday brunch. This is my fusion version of those two wonderful dishes, combining the spicy tomatoes, lamb and eggs.

Heat the oil in a large lidded pan over medium heat. Cook the onion until translucent, then add the garlic, salt and ground lamb.

Fry the lamb until browned, then add the tomato, tomato paste, spices and diced potatoes. Cook for a further 20 minutes over low heat. Add the peas. If it looks dry, add ¼ cup (60 ml) water.

Cook for a further 10 minutes until the sauce thickens and the potatoes are cooked.

Make 4–6 wells in the sauce and break an egg into each. Put the lid on and cook the egg to your liking.

Sprinkle with a handful of chopped cilantro and serve with kesra bread or naan.

Tip To make this dish vegetarian, swap the meat for a mixture of butternut squash and diced bell peppers (1 lb 2–5 oz/500–600 g combined). You can also swap the peas for red kidney beans and swap the cilantro for parsley.

Strawberry cheesecake pancakes

Serves 6

2 large eggs
2½ cups (600 ml) buttermilk
1 tbsp sugar
1 tsp vanilla extract
zest of ½ lemon
¾ cup (180 g) cream cheese, softened
2 cups (240 g) all-purpose flour
2 tsp baking powder
¼ tsp salt
1 cup (240 ml) strawberry jam
9 oz (250 g) fresh strawberries, hulled and halved
butter, for frying (optional)
confectioners' sugar
mascarpone or heavy cream, to serve

This is a delectable way to use up summer strawberries, so why not wow your family and friends with this stunner of a dish for brunch? These light and fluffy pancakes are filled with bursts of sweetness, making them the perfect weekend treat for a gathering.

Separate the eggs. Place the whites in one mixing bowl and yolks in another.

Add the buttermilk, sugar, vanilla and lemon zest to the yolks and mix to a smooth batter. Beat in the cream cheese, a little at a time, until well combined.

In a separate bowl, whisk the flour, baking powder and salt together then add to the buttermilk mixture, stirring until combined.

Using an electric mixer, whisk the egg whites with a pinch of salt until soft peaks form, then fold them into the batter.

In a large heatsafe bowl, heat the strawberry jam in the microwave just until melted. Add half of the strawberries to the jam and set aside.

Heat a nonstick frying pan over medium heat. You can add a little butter if you wish. Pour some of the batter into the pan and cook for 1–2 minutes. At this point you can add some fresh strawberries on top of the pancake; then flip it over so the strawberries are beneath and cooked into the batter. Fry until both sides are golden.

Drizzle the pancakes with strawberry sauce, dust with confectioners' sugar and serve with mascarpone or heavy cream.

Tip Make the pancakes any size you like. You can easily double the recipe and use any berries. If you want to leave the berries out of the pancakes, you can just serve them on the side.

Pav bhaji

Serves 4–6

for the bhaji
12 oz (350 g) potatoes, peeled and cut into chunks
3½ tbsp butter, plus 1–2 tbsp extra
1 tsp whole cumin seeds
1 large onion, chopped
14 oz (400 g) ripe tomatoes, chopped (or good-quality canned tomatoes)
1 tbsp tomato paste
2 tsp garam masala
1 tsp Kashmiri chile powder
1 tsp ground coriander
1 tsp amchur (mango powder)
1½ tsp salt
handful of chopped fresh cilantro, plus extra to serve

for serving
buttered fresh, soft bread rolls (slider buns work well)
1 red onion, thinly sliced
lime or lemon wedges, charred on a grill pan
tamarind chutney (see page 242), optional

This traditional Indian street-food dish is made of spiced mashed potatoes (bhaji) in a soft bread roll (pav). It is served by many street vendors and originated in Mumbai. This homemade version is a great way to enjoy this classic dish. You can add other vegetables like peas, grated carrot or small cauliflower florets—just reduce the potato to 7 oz (200 g) and make up the rest with your choice of vegetables.

Boil the potatoes in salty water until tender, 10–15 minutes. Drain well and then mash and set aside.

In a frying pan, heat 3½ tablespoons of butter and add the cumin seeds and onion. Fry until golden and soft. Add the chopped tomatoes and tomato paste and cook for 5 minutes. Then add all the spices, amchur and salt and cook over low heat until the oil separates, about 10 minutes.

Stir in the mashed potatoes. Cook for a further 10–15 minutes. The mixture needs to be a thick but loose consistency—not too runny. Add 1–2 tablespoons of butter and mix to combine. Stir in a handful of chopped cilantro.

Serve hot. I like to put a couple of spoonfuls in a buttered bread roll, topped with red onion, extra cilantro, a good squeeze of lime or lemon juice, and tamarind chutney if using.

Tip You can buy Kashmiri chile powder and amchur at Indian food stores. Kashmiri chile powder is less spicy than red chile powder and gives a lovely color to a dish without too much heat.

Smoked whole baby eggplants coated in spicy egg

Serves 4–6

4–6 baby or Japanese eggplants
olive oil
1 onion, thinly sliced
4–6 eggs, beaten
salt and ground black pepper
¼ tsp garam masala
½ tsp ground cumin
½ tsp ground coriander
1 tsp chile powder (or to taste)
handful of chopped fresh cilantro
roti or paratha (see page 241),
   or rice and salad, to serve
pomegranate seeds, to serve
small handful of fried
   curry leaves, to serve
chutney, to serve

A perfect brunch recipe. Once the eggplants are cooked, they become soft and velvety. Dipped in egg and cooked until golden, they make a great, nutritious start to your weekend.

Preheat your broiler to high. Line a baking sheet with parchment paper.

Wash and pat-dry the eggplants. Leaving the stems on, poke holes all over each eggplant with a fork. Place on the lined baking sheet and place under the broiler until softened and charred. You will have to keep turning them to cook them evenly.

While they are cooking, heat 1–2 tablespoons of oil in a frying pan and fry the sliced onion until golden. Set aside to cool slightly.

In a large, shallow bowl, whisk the eggs with salt and pepper and all the spices. Add the fried onion and chopped cilantro to the egg mixture.

When the eggplants are charred and feel soft, set them aside to cool. Once cooled, peel the skin off. Lay each eggplant on a chopping board and flatten gently with a fork so they are shaped like a teardrop.

Heat another 1–2 tablespoons of oil in the frying pan and then coat each eggplant well in the egg mixture. Cook until golden (2–3 minutes) and then flip with a spatula and cook the other side. Repeat with the rest of the eggplants.

Serve hot with roti or paratha, or rice and a salad. Top with pomegranate seeds, curry leaves and chutney.

Tip You can soften the eggplants directly on your stovetop if you have a gas burner—it gives a real charred finish (though personally I don't like to do this as I find it gets too messy). Use whatever seasoning you like. I have suggested one eggplant per person, but you can easily double the quantities to cook more.

Sweet & salty lassis

Each recipe serves 2

for the mango & cardamom lassi
2½ cups (500 g) mango pulp (fresh, canned or frozen)
2–3 green cardamom pods, seeds extracted and crushed
1 cup (250 ml) cold milk
1 cup (250 ml) plain yogurt
small handful of ice cubes
pinch saffron threads steeped in 1 tbsp water (optional)
crushed pistachios, to garnish
freeze-dried raspberries, to garnish
edible dried Persian rose petals, to garnish

for the salt lassi
½ tsp sea salt flakes
1⅔ cups (400 ml) plain yogurt
scant 1 cup (200 ml) water
small handful of ice cubes
1 tsp roasted cumin seeds, to garnish

for the rose lassi
2–3 tsp rose water
1 drop red food coloring (or less, depending on how pink you want it)
1 cup (250 ml) cold milk
1 cup (250 ml) plain yogurt
small handful of ice cubes
pomegranate seeds, to garnish

Lassi is easy to make and fabulous with any Indian meal. It's a blend of yogurt, salt, spices and water, and you can make sweet versions, too. It's known to help with the digestion of spicy foods. I love the salty version with a spicy curry. The sweet versions also make great summer smoothies.

For each lassi, combine all of the ingredients, except for the garnishes, in a blender, blend until smooth, and chill.

For the mango & cardamom lassi: Save the pistachios, raspberries and rose petals to sprinkle on top and serve.

For the salt lassi: Save the cumin seeds to sprinkle on top and serve.

For the rose lassi: Save the pomegranate seeds to sprinkle on top and serve.

Tip For a dairy-free option, use coconut milk and coconut yogurt.

Rose, apricot & honey iced tea

Serves 8

2 lb 4 oz (1 kg) fresh apricots, peeled and chopped
¾ cup (150 g) sugar
3–4 green tea bags
4 tbsp honey
2 tsp rose water
edible dried Persian rose petals, to garnish

This enticing iced tea is perfect to serve as part of a brunch menu or as a refreshing drink on a hot day. The floral taste with rose and honey just make this tea really special.

Purée the apricots in a blender with the sugar.

Bring 4¼ cups (1 liter) of water to a boil in a very large pot. Add the green tea bags and steep for 5 minutes, before removing.

Add the apricot purée, honey and rose water, stir to mix and leave to cool.

Once cool, strain the liquid and add 2–2½ cups (500–600 ml) water until diluted to your liking.

Serve in pretty little glasses with ice, and garnish with dried rose petals.

Tip You can use canned apricots for this recipe, if you wish, in which case you don't need to add the sugar.

Living in Malawi, with balmy weather most of the year, we loved eating alfresco, whether it was at a braai (barbecue), a picnic by the lake, or family gathering around the coal firepit, eating monkey nuts and corn freshly cooked on the hot coals. These recipes are designed to bring ease to outdoor entertaining.

Summer picnics & alfresco dining

Masala corn on the cob

Serves 3–6

3 corn cobs
2 tbsp oil
½ tsp chile powder
½ tsp salt
½ tsp chile flakes
1 tsp white vinegar

These masala corn on the cob are a favorite in our family. We grew up eating them and the highlight was always sitting around the firepit and getting our hands messy.

Remove the husks and silks from the corn. Boil in salty water until just tender. Cut each one in half. Set aside.

Alternatively, you can cook them in the microwave: remove a few of the outer husks. Place in microwave for 3 minutes per cob. Remove with a clean tea towel—it will be hot! Using a large sharp knife, slice ½ in (1 cm) off the stem end. Hold the silks and husks at the bottom end and gently squeeze the corn out of the husk. Voilà! No messy silks to deal with. Cut each cob in half.

In a deep-sided frying pan, add the oil, chile powder, salt, chile flakes and vinegar. Sizzle for about a minute, taking care not to burn the spices, then add the cooked corn on the cob pieces.

Turn to evenly coat the corn, and leave on the heat for a couple of minutes. Serve hot.

Tip You can par-cook the corn and then finish off on the grill, before you add them to the spicy sauce. You can also easily double the recipe to serve more people. If you are microwaving the corn, you can pull back the husks, remove the silks and then brush with the chile masala, leaving the husks attached when microwaving.

Spicy ground lamb & pea hand pies with chutney

Makes 20–24

1 tbsp olive oil
1 lb 2 oz (500 g) ground lamb
1 tsp ground cumin
1 tsp ground coriander
¾ tsp ground turmeric
salt and ground black pepper
½ cup (70 g) frozen peas
5–6 sheets store-bought puff pastry, partially defrosted
1 egg, beaten
handful of toasted cumin seeds
tomato chutney (see page 242), to serve

A favorite in our family, these hand pies are a picnic essential. Easy to make and very portable, I usually have some in the freezer to take out at short notice. Bake from frozen in 30 minutes and serve with your favorite chutney. These can be made vegetarian, too, by replacing the ground meat with potatoes, cauliflower or chickpeas.

Preheat the oven to 400°F (200°C). Line a baking sheet or sheets with parchment paper.

In a frying pan, heat the oil over medium heat and brown the ground lamb. Add the spices, seasoning and then the peas. Stir for a minute or two, then cover and cook over low heat until the meat is cooked through. The mixture should be quite dry but clinging together. You may need to add a splash of water if the meat is sticking to the pan. Leave the mixture to cool before making up the pies.

Once thawed, keep the pastry sheets covered with a tea towel while you work. Cut each sheet into four equal squares, and brush two adjacent sides with beaten egg (you will be bringing the corners together to make a triangle).

Spoon the filling onto the pastry. Make a triangle, pressing the sides down with a fork. Brush with egg, sprinkle with the toasted cumin seeds and arrange on prepared pan(s).

Bake the pies for 25–30 minutes or until puffed and golden.

Serve with chutney.

Tip Freeze the filled pies before baking, then bake from frozen (they may need a couple of minutes longer in the oven). I freeze them on a tray, then transfer them to freezer bags.

Koftas with marinated feta in thyme & chile oil

Serves 4–6

for the marinated feta
scant ½ cup (100 ml) olive oil
2 tbsp fresh thyme (or any herb you like; rosemary works well)
½ tsp chile flakes
2–3 garlic cloves, crushed
ground black pepper
14 oz (400 g) feta, cut into cubes
5¼ oz (150 g) sundried tomatoes in oil, drained, reserve the oil
3½ oz (100 g) olives of your choice

for the koftas
1 lb 2 oz (500 g) ground beef
½ cup (60 g) breadcrumbs
1 onion, finely chopped
2 green chiles, finely chopped (optional)
1 in (3 cm) fresh ginger, grated
2 tsp ground coriander
1 tsp ground cumin
½ tsp ground cinnamon
1 egg, beaten
salt and ground black pepper
neutral oil, for frying

for serving
pita bread or naan (see page 241), to serve
fresh thyme, to garnish
relish of your choice, to serve

Koftas are usually made with ground meat and can be skewered or made into balls. Traditionally infused with Indian or Middle Eastern spices, they are full of flavor. The marinated feta can be made a day or so ahead. These koftas are lovely served with pita bread or homemade naan (see page 241) and are easy to transport if you are planning a day out.

For the marinated feta: Mix together the oil and thyme in a large jar. Stir in the chile flakes, garlic and black pepper, then add the feta, tomatoes and olives (you can add some of the reserved oil, if you like). Screw on the lid and refrigerate overnight to marinate. I like to use a large jar because it's transportable if you are taking it to a picnic. Just make sure the lid is on tightly.

For the koftas: In a large bowl, mix the ground meat, breadcrumbs, onion, chiles, ginger, spices, egg and salt and pepper. Ensure the mixture is combined well. Shape into small balls, using the palm of your hands.

Heat the oil in a frying pan over medium heat and add the koftas, frying them until cooked through and brown on all sides. Drain on paper towels and set aside. You may need to cook the koftas in batches.

To toast the pita, heat a grill pan and brush with a little olive oil. Add the pita one at a time, flipping once toasty and slightly charred.

Place the koftas on a serving dish and scatter over the fresh thyme. Serve alongside the marinated feta, olives and tomatoes, relish and the pita bread.

Tip The koftas can be eaten warm or at room temperature.

Zucchini & corn sliders with mango chutney

Makes 12 large or 24 small fritters

2 corn cobs (or 1½ cups/225 g frozen corn kernels)
2 small zucchinis, grated
1 small onion, finely sliced
2 eggs, separated
½ cup (60 g) all-purpose flour
2 tbsp water
½ tsp ground cumin
salt and ground black pepper
2 tbsp oil

for the mango chutney
2 large mangoes, peeled, pit removed
2 tbsp lime juice
2 tbsp vegetable oil
½–1 tsp chile flakes
1 tsp cumin seeds
1 tsp coriander seeds
½ tsp mustard seeds
3 tbsp brown sugar (add another tbsp if you like it sweeter)
¾ cup (180 ml) white wine vinegar
salt and ground black pepper

for serving
slider buns
arugula or salad greens

A delicious combination, these fritters are great on their own or served in small slider buns with fresh lettuce and my luscious mango chutney. You can try grated carrot to replace the zucchini or grated broccoli stems if you prefer. A tasty treat for the whole family.

For the fritters: Trim the husks and silks from the corn. Using a sharp knife, cut the kernels from the cobs. Cook the corn in a small pot of salted boiling water until tender, then set aside.

Squeeze out the excess moisture from the grated zucchini.

In a bowl, combine the zucchini, corn, onion, egg yolks, flour and water. Add the cumin and salt and pepper.

In a separate bowl, beat the egg whites until peaks have formed. Fold the egg whites into the vegetable mixture. Shape mixture into 12 large or 24 small fritters.

Heat the oil in a large frying pan over medium heat. Cook the fritters in batches until golden and cooked through, about 2 minutes each side.

For the mango chutney: Dice the mangoes and squeeze lime juice over them. Toss and set aside.

In a pot, heat the oil and then add the spices. Cook for a few seconds, then add the sugar and white wine vinegar. Let it simmer for 7–8 minutes over low heat. Add the mango, season with salt and pepper and leave to cook for a further 7–8 minutes until the mango is silky and the liquid becomes syrupy. Leave to cool.

Serve the fritters in buns with fresh greens and a dollop of mango chutney.

Tip You can make the mango chutney ahead of time and store it in jars in the fridge for one week. Serve it at room temperature. The fritters can be made gluten free by swapping the all-purpose flour with rice flour. For some extra sauce, serve the sliders with Greek yogurt.

Tomato & goat cheese tart

Serves 6–8

for the tart base
1 cup (115 g) wholewheat flour
1 cup (115 g) rolled oats
½ cup (120 ml) neutral oil
½ cup (120 ml) cold water
½ tsp salt

for the filling
5 eggs
¾ cup (180 ml) heavy cream
¼ cup (25 g) grated Parmesan
14 oz (400 g) mixed heirloom tomatoes, sliced
3½ oz (100 g) soft goat cheese, crumbled
small handful of fresh basil leaves
drizzle of olive oil
pepper

This uses one of my favorite tart bases that I have used over and over again; the recipe was given to me by a woman I have known for 25 years, Jo, who I met while I was nursing her sick daughter in Wellington Hospital. She quickly became a very dear friend. Jo uses this base to make a lovely asparagus quiche. It's more nutritious than pastry, easy to make, has a lovely flavor and never feels too heavy.

Preheat the oven to 325°F (160°C). While the oven is heating up, make the tart base.

In a large bowl, mix together the flour, oats, oil, water and salt. If the mixture is too sticky, add a little more flour or oats.

Spread the dough into a quiche dish or 9 in (23 cm) loose-bottomed tart pan, making sure it goes up the sides. Place it in the oven to blind-bake for 15 minutes.

In a bowl, whisk the eggs, cream and Parmesan together.

Remove the tart base from the oven. Cover the base with tomato slices (reserving about a quarter them for later), pour in the egg mixture, and sprinkle the top with the goat cheese. Bake for 35–40 minutes or until set.

Just before serving, arrange the reserved tomato slices on top, scatter with basil leaves, drizzle with olive oil and sprinkle with black pepper.

Tip This can be served hot or at room temperature, so it's perfect for a picnic. (If you are taking it out, place the sliced tomatoes on when you get to your destination.)

Spiced pumpkin & sweet potato empanadas

Makes 18–20

for the pastry
4 cups (500 g) all-purpose flour
2 tsp baking powder
1 tsp salt
11 tbsp (150 g) cold unsalted butter

for the filling
9 oz (250 g) pumpkin and or butternut squash, peeled and chopped
9 oz (250 g) sweet potato, peeled and chopped
2 tbsp olive oil
2 tsp ground cumin
1 tsp ground coriander
salt and ground black pepper
1 small red onion, finely chopped
small handful of chopped fresh cilantro
⅔ cup (75 g) crumbled feta
1 egg, lightly beaten
sesame seeds
mango chutney (page 60), to serve

A great recipe to have in your repertoire. To make it even easier, you can use store-bought shortcrust pastry if you don't want to make your own. And you can make the filling for these a day ahead and refrigerate it until needed. The empanadas can also be frozen on the day you assemble them and then cooked from frozen when needed.

Preheat the oven to 400°F (200°C).

To make the pastry, combine the flour, baking powder and salt in a large bowl. Grate the butter into the bowl and rub into the mix until it resembles breadcrumbs. Mix in just enough cold water to bring it together, then wrap in plastic wrap or a beeswax wrap and pop in the fridge for an hour.

Meanwhile, combine the pumpkin and sweet potato with the oil and spices and place on a large roasting pan. Season with salt and pepper. Roast, turning occasionally, for 20 minutes or until cooked through.

Transfer to a heatproof bowl and mash. Stir in the onion, cilantro and feta. Put in the fridge until cooled.

When you're ready to bake the empanadas, preheat the oven to 400°F (200°C).

Divide the pastry dough into 18–20 balls. Roll each ball into a 4 in (10 cm) circle (you can use a cookie cutter for a uniform shape, but I like mine rustic). Spoon 1 tablespoon of the filling onto one half of each circle. Brush the edges with a little beaten egg and fold the dough over tightly to enclose the filling and form a half-moon shape. Twist and fold the edge to seal in the filling.

Place the empanadas on baking sheets, brush with beaten egg, sprinkle with sesame seeds and bake for 30 minutes until golden.

Serve hot or at room temperature with mango chutney.

Tip Freeze the filled empanadas before baking, then bake from frozen (they may need a couple of minutes longer in the oven). I freeze them on a tray, then transfer them to freezer bags once partially frozen, to prevent them from sticking together.

Hot-smoked salmon quiche

Serves 4

2 large sheets store-bought puff pastry
oil, for frying
1 small onion, finely chopped
1 tsp Dijon mustard
10½ oz (300 g) hot-smoked salmon
5 eggs
¾ cup (180 ml) heavy cream
¾ cup (180 ml) milk
1 cup (115 g) grated cheese
salt and ground black pepper

Quiche is one of those dishes you can throw together with anything you have in the fridge. It's a perfect food for picnics and eating alfresco. It can be eaten hot or cold and served with a crunchy salad and homemade chutney. I've made this using home-smoked salmon (see page 156) but you could use store-bought.

Preheat the oven to 350°F (180°C).

Line a 9 in (23 cm) pie dish with puff pastry, cutting the sheets to fit. Fill with pie weights (or dried beans or rice) and blind bake for 10–12 minutes.

Meanwhile, add a splash of oil to a frying pan over medium heat and sauté the onion until soft and golden. Add the mustard and salmon; stir for 2–3 minutes, and then turn off the heat.

In a large bowl, whisk together the eggs, cream, milk and cheese and season with salt and pepper.

Scatter the salmon and onion mixture over the pastry, and pour on the egg mixture, making sure the salmon is spread around evenly.

Bake for 30–40 minutes until the egg is set.

Serve with a zesty salad.

Mixed heirloom tomato & labneh salad

Serves 4–6

for the labneh
1 tsp sea salt flakes
2 cups (500 g) Greek-style yogurt

for the dressing
¼ cup (60 ml) extra virgin olive oil
1½ tbsp lemon juice
1 garlic clove, quartered
pinch of chile flakes (optional)
salt and ground black pepper

for the salad
2 tbsp chopped pistachios
2 tsp pumpkin seeds
2 tsp sesame seeds
2 tsp ground cumin
1 tsp sea salt flakes
2 lb 4 oz (1 kg) mixed heirloom tomatoes
½ cup (65 g) green or kalamata olives, pitted, sliced if you wish
small red onion, sliced into rounds
3 cups (100 g) watercress, arugula, or nasturtium
1 cup (16 g) fresh cilantro leaves
crusty bread, to serve

Labneh is a thick, creamy yogurt from which the whey has been strained. It's a Middle Eastern staple and can be used in salads, or as a dip, drizzled with olive oil and dukkah. You will need to make the labneh and dressing ahead of time—at least a day before would be best.

For the labneh: Stir the salt through the Greek yogurt. Arrange a large piece of cheeesecloth in a deep bowl. Place the yogurt on the cloth. Take a wooden spoon and rest it across the top of the bowl. Tie the ends of the cloth to the wooden spoon—the weight of the mixture will help drain the liquid. Refrigerate for 24–48 hours, gently squeezing to encourage the liquid to drain. When enough of the liquid has drained, you should be able to shape the labneh into a log or balls.

For the dressing: Combine all the ingredients in a screw-top jar and shake to combine. Place in the fridge for 24 hours. Discard the garlic before use.

For the salad: In a dry frying pan, toast the pistachios, seeds, spices and salt until fragrant. Remove and set aside to cool.

Halve the smaller tomatoes and thickly slice the larger ones; arrange on a large platter.

In a bowl, combine the olives, red onion, the watercress, arugula, or nasturtium, and the cilantro. Pour over half of the dressing and gently toss to combine.

Scatter the salad mixture over the tomatoes and top with the labneh (either balls or cut into slices if you rolled it). Sprinkle with toasted pistachios, seeds and spices and drizzle over the rest of the dressing.

Serve with crusty bread.

Anj's chicken sharwama in naan with pickled onions

Serves 6–8

2 lb 4 oz (1 kg) boneless chicken thighs or breasts
1 tbsp vinegar
1 tsp salt
ground black pepper
handful of fresh cilantro
1–2 green chiles
2 tbsp olive oil
1 onion, finely sliced
1 tsp ground cumin
3–4 garlic cloves, crushed
naan (see page 241) or toasted pita
tamarind chutney (see page 242)
plain yogurt

for the pickled onions
1 cup (240 ml) water
1 cup (240 ml) white wine vinegar or white vinegar
1 tbsp salt
¼ cup (50 g) sugar
2 red onions, thinly sliced (a mandolin works well)
2 green chiles, thinly sliced (optional)
½ tbsp black or pink peppercorns

This is my twin sister Anjum's recipe. She has a family of six, and she's always busy with work and afterschool activities with her youngest, so easy, quick and nutritious meals are key. I love serving these in separate bowls so everyone can make their own.

In a large pot, combine the chicken with the vinegar, salt and pepper and boil for 20–30 minutes until tender. Once tender, remove from the pot, reserving some of the stock. Shred the chicken with a fork.

In a blender, blend the cilantro and green chiles. Set aside.

Heat the oil in a large frying pan and fry the onion until slightly golden. Add some salt and pepper, and the cumin, garlic, and cilantro-chile mixture. Next add the shredded chicken with a little of the stock—you don't want it too runny, just enough for the chicken not to dry out. Simmer for a few minutes. Set aside.

For the pickled onions: Heat the water, vinegar, salt and sugar in a saucepan over medium heat, until the salt and sugar have dissolved. Set aside to cool. In a 1 pint (500 ml) jar, combine the onions, chiles and peppercorns. Add the vinegar mixture to the jar. Allow to cool before sealing. Once the pickled onions are tender and bright pink they are ready to use. They will keep in the fridge for a week or so.

Serve the sharwama in naan or toasted pita bread, topped with pickled onions, chutney and a dollop of yogurt.

Middle Eastern salad with pomegranate dressing

Serves 6–8

1 eggplant, cut into ½ in (1 cm) cubes
4 tbsp olive oil, plus extra for drizzling
3 flatbreads, like pita or naan (see page 241), cut into small squares
salt and ground black pepper
3 bell peppers (red, yellow and green), deseeded and cut into ½ in (1 cm) cubes
2 large tomatoes, diced
3–4 scallions, sliced
small bunch of flat-leaf parsley, chopped
¼ cup mint leaves, chopped
seeds of ½ pomegranate

for the pomegranate dressing
3 tbsp pomegranate molasses
3 tbsp olive oil
juice of ½ lemon
2 tsp brown sugar
salt and ground black pepper

This colorful salad is a great way to feed a crowd. It works perfectly as part of a menu or as a meal on its own. The recipe was originally given to me by my sister Farha, who lives in the UAE, and I make it often. The dressing is one of my favorites, so I use it in other salads, too.

Preheat the oven to 400°F (200°C).

Spread the eggplant cubes on a baking sheet, drizzle with a little olive oil and bake until golden and crisp, 12–15 minutes.

Heat the olive oil in a frying pan, add flatbread pieces and fry in batches until golden. Season with salt and pepper and set aside on a plate lined with paper towels.

In a large salad bowl, combine the eggplant cubes, bell peppers, tomatoes, scallions, parsley and mint. Toss together.

Place all the dressing ingredients in a jar, season with salt and pepper and shake to combine. Pour the dressing over the salad and toss again.

Top the salad with the flatbread pieces just before serving, so they remain crisp. Garnish with pomegranate seeds.

I love vegetables. All of my cookbooks have a good selection of vegetarian options, but for this book I decided to give them a whole chapter. This chapter is all about great seasonal vegetables with lots of flavor, enhanced by spices and pantry staples. It is not entirely vegan, as I do use eggs and dairy in some of my recipes, but you can always use your favorite plant-based substitutes. As you cook these dishes, you will discover flavor pairings you may not have tried before. These recipes are easy and vibrant and, like most of my cooking, a mix of East and West.

Glorious vegetables

Spice-roasted vegetables with haloumi & a cilantro-chile dressing

Serves 6–8

2 parsnips
2 beets
2 sweet potatoes
3 carrots
3 tbsp olive oil
1 tsp ground cumin
½ tsp ground coriander
½ tsp garam masala
salt and ground black pepper
7 oz (200 g) haloumi or paneer
neutral oil, for frying
fresh lettuce leaves

for the cilantro-chile dressing
¼ cup (60 ml) olive oil
3 tbsp chopped fresh cilantro
juice of ½ lemon
2 tsp honey
1 tsp balsamic vinegar
1 garlic clove, crushed
1 tsp chile flakes
salt and ground black pepper

This colorful salad is a feast for the eyes. Full of veggie goodness, the sweetness and spice are beautifully balanced with the fresh dressing that has a slight kick to round things out.

Preheat the oven to 400°F (200°C).

Peel and chop vegetables into ¾ in (2 cm) chunks. Place in a large baking dish.

In a small bowl, whisk together the olive oil, spices, salt and pepper. Drizzle over the vegetables, coating them well. Roast in the oven for about 45 minutes until cooked and golden.

Meanwhile, thinly slice the haloumi and pat dry with paper towels.

Heat a lightly oiled nonstick frying pan over medium heat and cook the haloumi until golden on both sides. Set aside to cool.

Combine all the dressing ingredients together in a small blender, blend, and season with salt and pepper. You can add a dash more salt, lemon juice or chile according to your taste.

Once vegetables are cooked, cool to room temperature then assemble your salad.

Place the lettuce leaves in a large dish with the roasted vegetables and mix gently. Scatter haloumi on top and drizzle with the dressing.

Spinach, feta & pine nut tart

Serves 6

14 oz (400 g) store-bought shortcrust pastry
1 lb 2 oz (500 g) baby spinach
3½ tbsp butter
salt and ground black pepper
1¼ cups (300 ml) heavy cream
6 egg yolks
9 oz (250 g) feta
⅔ cup (100 g) pine nuts

Tarts are a food of variety and possibility; they can be simple and rustic or elegant and refined. Either way they are always a pleasure to eat. I have a few in this cookbook, and while it's lovely to be able to make the pastry, you don't have to—sometimes you just want quick and easy. With the busy lives we all lead, store-bought pastry is an easy option.

Preheat the oven to 400°F (200°C).

On a lightly floured work surface, roll the pastry out to about ½ in (1.5 cm) thick (if it is not already rolled). Line a 9 in (23 cm) flan dish or tart pan with the pastry, cutting it to fit. Fill the base with pie weights (or dried beans or rice) and blind bake for 10 minutes.

Bring a pot of water to a boil. Blanch the spinach in the boiling water for 1 minute and then drain. Press to squeeze all the water out. Coarsely chop the spinach.

Melt the butter in a frying pan, add the spinach and cook gently to evaporate any remaining liquid. Season with salt and pepper. Stir in the cream and egg yolks.

Crumble the feta on the pie crust, top with the creamed spinach and bake for 15 minutes. Scatter the pine nuts on top and cook for a further 5 minutes until golden brown.

Tip You can use the leftover egg whites for my baked Alaska (see page 199) or peach meringue cake (see page 193).

Fried harissa-spiced eggplants with a sizzling chile yogurt

Serves 4–6

for the eggplants
2 large eggplants
neutral oil, for frying
1 tbsp rose harissa paste
¼ cup (60 ml) pomegranate molasses
1 tbsp honey
pomegranate seeds

for the sizzling chile yogurt
2 cups (480 g) plain yogurt (I like to use Greek)
2–3 scallions, chopped
½ cup (8 g) chopped fresh cilantro
½ cup (70 g) pine nuts
1 tsp salt
½ tsp chile flakes
¼ cup (60 ml) peanut oil

As a child I absolutely hated eggplant; the cooked texture put me right off! But as an adult I love it and cook with it whenever I can. Once cooked, it becomes luscious and velvety, and in this dish I have paired it with harissa and yogurt for an amazing combination.

Slice the eggplants into ½ in (1 cm) rounds (keep the skin on) and score each slice. Fry in oil until nearly cooked then set aside on a baking sheet lined with parchment paper.

In a bowl, whisk together the rose harissa, pomegranate molasses and honey. Brush this over the eggplant slices and broil in the oven for 4–6 minutes until lightly colored.

Spread the yogurt in a shallow dish. In a separate bowl, combine the scallions, cilantro, pine nuts, salt and chile flakes.

Heat the peanut oil in a small pan until hot (not smoking). Pour it into the scallion mixture—it should sizzle. Immediately pour this onto the yogurt.

Arrange the eggplants on a serving platter, scatter over the pomegranate seeds and serve with the yogurt.

Tip Rose harissa paste can be found in specialty food stores. You can also use plain harissa paste, without the rose.

Egg curry with paratha

Serves 2

1 tbsp oil
2 tbsp tomato passata or sauce
1 tbsp tomato paste
1 tsp chile powder
1 tsp ground coriander
½ tsp ground turmeric
½ tsp ground cumin
3 hard-boiled eggs, shelled and halved lengthways

for serving
handful of chopped fresh cilantro
paratha or roti (see page 241), or store-bought
cucumber raita (see page 242)

You know what they say, if you have eggs in the house, you will never go hungry. When we lived in Malawi, we had chickens, so we always had eggs, fresh and totally free range. My family love eggs and we all eat them differently. I love them fried with onions; my husband Graham likes boiled or poached; my daughter Zara makes a mean cheese omelet, and my son Adam loves his scrambled. This very easy curry is so quick it's perfect for a lunch or last-minute weeknight supper.

Heat the oil in a pot over medium heat. Add the tomato passata, tomato paste, and then the spices and cook over low heat until the oil looks like it is separating from the tomato mixture.

Place the hard-boiled eggs in the tomato mixture and cook over low heat for 5 minutes. Don't stir too much as you will break the eggs, but you can spoon the sauce over the eggs until it is all combined.

Top with the fresh cilantro and serve with paratha or roti and cucumber raita.

Roasted sweet potatoes with curry leaf & mustard seed yogurt

Serves 4–6

2 lb 4 oz (1 kg) sweet potatoes (I use all the varieties I can find)
1 small star anise
½ tsp cumin seeds
1 tsp ground cinnamon
½ tsp chile powder
½ tsp amchur (mango powder)
2 tbsp olive oil
sea salt and ground black pepper
1–2 tbsp oil
1 tsp mustard seeds
8–10 curry leaves
1 cup (240 ml) plain yogurt
handful of fried curry leaves
handful of chopped fresh cilantro (optional)
lime or lemon wedges (optional)

This is a gorgeous dish—the sweetness of the sweet potato paired with the spices and the tanginess of the mango powder, all drizzled with the yogurt, create layers of flavor. The fried curry leaves add a crispy element that works wonderfully.

Preheat the oven to 350°F (180°C).

Peel the sweet potatoes, cut each in half lengthways, and then into 2 or 3 wedges (depending on their size) so you have 4–5 large wedges from each one. Arrange on a roasting pan.

In a spice grinder or using a mortar and pestle, grind the whole spices until powdered. Place them in a small bowl and add the remaining spices, amchur, olive oil and a good sprinkle of salt and pepper. Mix well and drizzle the mixture over the wedges.

Roast the wedges for 30–35 minutes or until tender and golden. Once they are cooked, arrange them on a platter and set aside.

Heat the oil in a small pan, and add the mustard seeds and curry leaves. Once they start popping, pour them on top of the yogurt.

Dollop the yogurt over the sweet potatoes, sprinkle with chopped cilantro and serve with lime or lemon wedges.

Kokum batata with bhel

Serves 4–6

for the tamarind sauce
3 tsp tamarind paste
4 tsp brown sugar
½ tsp ground cumin
⅓ cup (75 ml) water

for the kokum batata
1 tbsp oil
handful of curry leaves
1 tsp mustard seeds
¾ cup (200 g) tomato sauce
½ tsp salt
1 tsp chile powder
1 tsp ground paprika
2 green chiles, chopped (optional)
1 tbsp tomato paste
1 tbsp ketchup
1 tsp white vinegar
1 lb 2 oz (500 g) baby potatoes
14 oz (400 g) cooked chickpeas (rinsed and drained if using canned)

for the bhel
small bunch of chopped fresh cilantro
1 small red onion, chopped (optional)
pomegranate seeds
handful of Bombay or bhuja mix

A scrumptious snack in a bowl, full of vibrant flavors and textures. It's a dish that was always served to visitors for afternoon tea when I was a child. Kokum means tamarind and batata means potato. Bhel is a mixture of Bombay or bhuja mix and fresh ingredients like onion, cilantro, and pomegranate seeds. I sometimes make this dish if I'm cooking just for myself and don't feel like a big meal. It's spicy, crunchy and tangy—a bowl full of goodness. It tastes even better the next day.

For the tamarind sauce: Simmer all the ingredients together in a small saucepan until the sauce thickens. Allow to cool before serving. (This sauce tastes better the next day and keeps well in the fridge for up to 1 month.)

For the kokum batata: Heat the oil in a large pot, and add the curry leaves and mustard seeds. Once the seeds start popping, add the tomato sauce, salt, chile powder, paprika and green chiles (if using) and cook for 2–3 minutes over medium heat.

Stir in the tomato paste, ketchup and vinegar and continue cooking over low heat for 10 minutes.

Meanwhile, peel the potatoes if you like (don't bother peeling if they are new potatoes) and cut into halves or quarters, depending on size. Parboil for 8–10 minutes, then drain.

Take a small handful of the potatoes and roughly mash them. Add these to the tomato mixture, along with the remaining potatoes and chickpeas. Simmer for a further 8–10 minutes.

Place into small bowls with the cilantro and red onion sprinkled on top. Scatter with the pomegranate seeds. Drizzle liberally with tamarind sauce and serve with crunchy Bombay mix.

Tip The Bombay or bhuja mix topping can be found in any South Asian supermarket.

Harissa spice-crusted paneer & mango salad

Serves 4–6

for the salad
- 10–14 oz (300–400 g) block of paneer cheese
- 1–2 tbsp harissa paste
- 2 cups (60 g) baby spinach and/or mixed salad greens
- 2 large ripe mangoes, cheeks cut into ¾ in (2 cm) cubes
- ½ small red onion, finely sliced
- handful of roasted peanuts

for the cilantro and chile dressing
- 4–5 tbsp olive oil
- 1 tsp balsamic vinegar
- juice of ½ lemon
- 3 tbsp chopped fresh cilantro
- 2 tsp liquid honey
- 1–2 garlic cloves, crushed
- 1 tsp chile flakes
- salt and ground black pepper

I love putting this salad together. Mangoes are one of my favorite fruits—we grew up eating them peeled whole and then biting off chunks until we got to the large seed, enjoying every sweet bit of flesh until we had mango juice dripping down our chins and hands. Pairing this with harissa—a North African paste made from garlic, spices, dried red chile and oil—is an amazing combination.

For the salad: Cut the block of paneer into ½ in (1 cm) slices. Place the harissa in a small bowl.

Heat a dry nonstick frying pan and dry fry one side of the cheese slices until golden, turn over and, using a pastry brush, brush the harissa over the cooked side.

Fry the other side until golden, turn over and brush on the harissa—only give them 30 seconds or so once you have put the harissa on as you don't want the harissa to burn. Set aside.

For the dressing: Combine all the ingredients in a jar and shake together. You can also blend together in a blender if you prefer.

In a serving bowl, combine the spinach and mixed salad greens. Arrange the mangoes, red onion and spiced paneer on top. Drizzle with the dressing, sprinkle with the peanuts and serve.

Stuffed naan with turmeric apple achaar

Makes 16–18 naan
Makes 1¼ cups (300 ml) achaar

for the turmeric apple achaar
2 cooking apples, diced
1 tsp ground turmeric
1 tsp salt
2 tbsp oil
¼ tsp cumin seeds
¼ tsp fenugreek seeds
¼ tsp nigella seeds
¼ tsp mustard seeds
¼ tsp fennel seeds
1–2 whole cloves
3–4 curry leaves
1 tbsp grated ginger
1 tbsp grated garlic
3 tbsp soft brown sugar or jaggery (if you can get it)
3 tbsp white vinegar

for the naan
4 cups (480 g) self-rising flour
1½ tsp salt
2 cups (480 g) plain yogurt
olive oil, for frying

for the filling
1 cup (100 g) chopped scallions
1 cup (16 g) chopped fresh cilantro
½ tsp ground coriander
½ tsp ground cumin
1 tbsp oil

The best-ever naan! I make them often as they're so easy to throw together, and no yeast needed. You can leave them plain or stuff them. I like to use a little oil to cook them as it gives a lovely glossy finish. Growing up in Malawi, my mom and aunt used to make achaars and pickles (mango, lemon, apple) to store away for the year.

For the achaar: Put the apples in a sieve lined with cheesecloth and set over a bowl. Add the turmeric and salt and leave overnight.

Heat the oil in a shallow pan over medium heat and fry the seeds and cloves. Once they start popping, add the curry leaves, ginger and garlic and stir. Add the sugar and vinegar, bring to a boil and then simmer until the vinegar has reduced. Add the apples and mix to coat.

Spoon into sterilized jar(s) and allow to cool fully before refrigerating. The achaar should keep in the fridge for 1 week.

For the naan: Mix the flour and salt together in a bowl. Pour in the yogurt and mix until just combined. Divide the dough into 16–18 pieces.

In a separate bowl, mix all the filling ingredients together.

Using floured hands, flatten each piece of dough into a round. Place a spoonful of filling in the center and bring the edges into the middle. Pinch to close, forming a parcel. Set aside until all are filled.

Gently roll the parcels out ito 5–5½ in (12–14 cm) rounds.

Preheat a nonstick frying pan over medium heat. Add a splash of olive oil to the pan and cook each naan until both sides are golden, pillowy and cooked through—a couple of minutes on each side.

Tip The naan can be stuffed with cheese, cooked ground meat, any greens, a spice mixture, or left plain. You can also cook them on a grill. You can make the achaar with green mangoes, as we did growing up, but they are harder to source. Jaggery is an unrefined sugar made from sugar cane or palm and can be found in South Asian grocery stores.

Gunpowder masala crispy choux potatoes

Serves 4 as a side dish

14 oz (400 g) red potatoes
3½ tbsp milk
2 tbsp butter
½ tsp garam masala
1 tsp chile powder
½ tsp chile flakes
1 tsp ground cumin
½ tsp ground cinnamon
½ tsp salt
½ tsp ground black pepper
neutral oil, for frying

for the choux pastry
½ cup (125 ml) water
3½ tbsp butter
½ tsp salt
⅔ cup (75 g) all-purpose flour
2 eggs

Few things compare to the pleasure of fried potatoes. I've taken them up a notch and given this traditionally French recipe of pommes dauphine an Indian spice boost—gunpowder is a hot South Indian spice blend. The result is a delicate crusty exterior and a luscious creamy center. These are oh-so addictive!

Peel and cut the potatoes in half. Add them to a pot of cold water with salt and boil until the potatoes are soft. Drain, then add the milk, butter, spices and salt and pepper. Mash, then set aside to cool.

For the choux pastry: In a pot over medium–high heat, bring the water, butter and salt to a boil then add the flour and mix until a ball forms. Cook for 5–7 minutes until it leaves the sides of the pot.

Take off the heat and cool. Transfer the dough to a stand mixer fitted with a paddle attachment, if you have one, and mix a little before adding the eggs one at a time, beating until they are fully incorporated and you have a glossy mixture. Alternatively, you can do this by hand with a wooden spoon.

Add the choux mixture to the mashed potatoes and stir until combined.

Heat the oil (about 2½ in/6 cm deep) in a wok or a large pot over medium heat. To check if the oil is hot enough, add a small piece of bread—if it turns golden, the oil is ready.

Drop small spoonfuls of the potato mixture into the oil and cook on both sides, flipping with a fork, until golden, puffy and cooked through. Make sure the oil isn't too hot or they will turn dark brown quickly and the insides won't be cooked. Remove with a slotted spoon and drain on paper towels. Fry in batches.

Sprinkle over extra chile flakes and salt. You can serve these on their own with a dipping sauce and lime wedges or as a side to any meat dish.

Cassava & vegetable stew

Serves 4–6

1 lb 2 oz (500 g) fresh or frozen cassava (yuca), in chunks
2–3 tbsp oil
2 onions, sliced
1 tsp salt
2 garlic cloves, crushed
1 tsp chile powder
½ tsp ground turmeric
½ tsp ground coriander
½ tsp ground paprika
¼ tsp ground cumin
3 tbsp tomato passata or puréed tomatoes
1 tbsp tomato paste
3 carrots, peeled and sliced
1 cup (90 g) broccoli florets
½ cabbage, cut into chunks
½ cup (70 g) frozen peas
1⅔ cups (400 ml) water
chopped cilantro, to serve
lemon wedges, to serve
crispy salad or crusty bread, to serve

We grew up eating cassava, a root vegetable similar to potato, in Malawi. It's a good source of resistant starch that supports gut health and blood sugar management. My mom loves making this wholesome stew with chunky vegetables and the starchy cassava. It's all your five-a-day in a healthy and nutritious meal.

Place the cassava in a pot, add just enough water to cover, and bring to a boil. Cook until soft, 15–20 minutes.

While the cassava is boiling, heat the oil in a large pot. Add the onions and cook until translucent, then add salt and garlic and cook for a further 2–3 minutes.

Add the chile, turmeric, coriander, paprika, cumin, tomato passata and tomato paste, stirring to make sure it is well combined.

Add the carrots, broccoli, cabbage, peas and water to the pot and cook over low heat until vegetables are tender, 20–30 minutes.

When the cassava is cooked (it should be soft), use a potato masher to mash it roughly in the water it was boiled in. You should have a chunky, starchy mash. Remove any stringy bits from the middle of the cassava as it breaks up.

Add the cassava to the vegetables and stir well to mix. Garnish with chopped cilantro. Serve immediately in a bowl with lemon wedges and a crispy salad or some crusty bread.

Tip You can find cassava in some supermarkets, or at Indian, Pacific, or Latin American grocery stores.

Peach, honey, goat cheese & chile salad

Serves 4

for the balsamic syrup
½ cup (120 ml) white wine vinegar
2 tbsp balsamic vinegar
¼ tsp chile flakes

for the salad
2–3 firm ripe peaches
1 tbsp honey
2 large handfuls arugula leaves
2 tbsp pickled onion (see page 20)
3½–5¼ oz (100–150 g) soft goat cheese
¼ cup (35 g) pine nuts, toasted (optional)
edible flowers (optional)

A quick and easy, sweet and salty salad that's perfect for summer. The pickled onion gives it a lovely crunch and bite and it looks so pretty with all the colors.

For the syrup: In a small pot, bring the vinegars to a boil. Reduce the heat and simmer until the mixture coats the back of the spoon, about 8 minutes. Add the chile flakes, stir and set aside to cool.

For the salad: Cut the peaches into thin wedges, place them in a bowl and drizzle with the honey.

Arrange the arugula on a platter and drizzle over some of the syrup. Arrange the peaches and pickled onion on top and crumble over the goat cheese. Drizzle again with the remaining syrup, scatter over the pine nuts and top with edible flowers (if using).

Tip If using 3 peaches, or large peaches, be sure to use the larger quantity of goat cheese.

Spicy kidney beans with rice

Serves 2–4

1 cup (200 g) basmati rice
2 tbsp oil
2 tsp salt
1 tsp grated ginger or ginger paste
1–2 garlic cloves, crushed
1 onion, finely sliced
1–2 green cardamom pods
1 bay leaf
1 cinnamon stick
14 oz (400 g) can whole tomatoes
1 tbsp tomato paste
1 tsp ground cumin
1 tsp Kashmiri chile powder
14 oz (400 g) can kidney beans
1 tsp garam masala
2 tbsp butter or vegan alternative
red onion, sliced
fried curry leaves, to garnish
lime wedges

An easy rescue curry that uses your pantry staples when there is nothing left in the fridge. This dish is delicious and filling. It's healthy and vegan-friendly, too.

For the rice: Wash the rice a couple of times until the water runs clear. Heat 1 tablespoon of oil in a saucepan with a lid and add the washed rice. Fry the rice for 1–2 minutes then add 2 cups (480 ml) of water and 1 teaspoon of the salt. Bring to a boil then reduce temperature to low. Cover and cook for 14–16 minutes.

Heat the remaining oil in a medium pot, add the ginger and garlic and sauté for 2–3 minutes. Add the onion and cook until translucent. Add the whole spices and cook for a minute. Stir in the tomatoes and tomato paste then add the cumin, chile and remaining salt. Cook over low heat until the oil separates.

Pour in the kidney beans, including the liquid, and simmer over low heat until the sauce is thick, about 15 minutes.

Stir through the garam masala and butter and garnish with red onion and curry leaves. Serve with plain rice and a lime wedge.

Tip You can buy Kashmiri chile powder at Indian grocery stores. It is less spicy than red chile powder and gives a lovely color to a dish without too much heat.

Chile & Parmesan smashed potatoes

Serves 4–6

2 lb 4 oz (1 kg) small potatoes (any roasting variety)
1 tbsp butter, melted
dash of olive oil
½ tsp chile flakes (optional)
½ tsp garlic powder
salt and ground black pepper
½ cup (50 g) grated Parmesan
handful of chopped fresh parsley or cilantro

This is a delicious way to spice up potatoes. Great as a side dish to any main or as part of a tapas menu, they are sure to impress your guests.

Wash and halve the potatoes lengthways, leaving the skin on.

Place the potatoes in a large pot, cover with water, add a pinch of salt and parboil for about 10 minutes—you don't want to overcook them. You can do this the night before, too.

Drain the potatoes and add the melted butter, olive oil, chile flakes (if using), garlic powder and salt and pepper. Stir gently to coat.

Preheat the oven to 350°F (180°C).

Sprinkle the Parmesan on a baking sheet. Place the potatoes cut-side down on top of the Parmesan and give each one a gentle "smash" with a fork or the bottom of a small glass.

Bake for 25–30 minutes until golden.

Garnish with parsley or cilantro. Eat these on their own or as a side to your favorite main dish.

Kitchari with pea & green bean curry

Serves 4–6

for the kitchari
1 cup (200 g) basmati rice
¼ cup (50 g) split black lentils
1 tbsp ghee
2 cups (480 ml) water
¾ tsp salt

for the pea & green bean curry
1 tbsp oil
¾ tsp ground coriander
½ tsp ground cumin
½ tsp chile powder or Kashmiri chile powder
½ tsp ground paprika
¼ tsp ground turmeric
a good grind of black pepper
½ tsp salt
¾ cup (200 g) canned whole tomatoes
1 tbsp tomato paste
9 oz (250 g) fresh (or frozen) green beans
½ cup (70 g) frozen peas

for the yogurt curry sauce
1 cup (240 ml) plain yogurt
1 cup (240 ml) water, plus 1 tbsp
1 tbsp chickpea (gram) flour
1 tbsp oil
3–4 fresh curry leaves
½ tsp chile powder
½ tsp ground coriander
¼ tsp ground turmeric
¼ tsp salt
1 tsp tomato paste
fried curry leaves, to garnish

This is one of my absolute favorite curry combinations. I have a meat version in my first cookbook *Ashia's Table*. I love this vegetarian version, too. It's my hug in a bowl. Once cooked, the plating is important. You start with the kitchari, add the pea and green bean curry and then a drizzle of the yogurt curry sauce. So good.

For the kitchari: Soak the rice and lentils together in water for 20–30 minutes. Drain then wash until the water runs clear.

In a lidded pot, heat the ghee and add the rice and lentils. Cook for a couple of minutes and then add the water and salt. Bring to a boil and then reduce the heat to its lowest setting, cover and leave to cook for approximately 15 minutes, until the water has been absorbed and the rice is cooked.

For the curry: Heat the oil in a pot over medium–high heat. Add all the spices and salt; stir and quickly add the tomatoes and tomato paste (you don't want the spices to burn). Turn the heat to low and put the lid on. Cook for 8–10 minutes.

Trim the ends off the the green beans. You can then microwave them for 5–6 minutes so they cook quicker, if you wish.

Add the green beans and then the peas to the curry. Cook over low heat until the beans and peas are cooked. Set aside.

For the yogurt curry sauce: In a bowl, whisk together the yogurt, 1 cup (240 ml) of the water and the chickpea flour. Set aside.

Heat the oil in a pot and add the curry leaves, then add all the spices, salt, tomato paste and 1 tablespoon of water. Cook for a couple of minutes. Add the yogurt mixture and cook for 6–7 minutes, stirring all the time. The sauce should turn a lovely golden color.

To serve, plate your kitchari, top with the pea and green bean curry and then pour over the yogurt sauce. Garnish with fried curry leaves.

This is one of my favorite chapters in this book. For me, gathering family and friends at the table, sharing the joy of food together, is one of life's most treasured things. Whether you are sitting outside under dusk light or inside with candles flickering everywhere, these are the moments to be savored and celebrated.

These recipes are made to be shared with your loved ones. From slow-cooked lamb that melts in your mouth to the sweet and savory crunch of a North African bastilla pie, this chapter spans across India, the Middle East and Africa. A world of flavors right here at your table.

Elaborate dinners & festive feasts

Baked beet & maple-glazed side of salmon

Serves 8-10

- 2 lb 2 oz–2 lb 10 oz (1–1.2 kg) side of salmon, skin on and boneless
- ½ cup (145 g) salt
- ¼ cup (50 g) raw sugar
- 2 tbsp whole coriander seeds, lightly crushed
- zest of 2 oranges
- 3 small beets, grated, plus a little extra to garnish
- ½ cup (160 g) maple syrup
- drizzle of oil
- fresh lettuce leaves, to serve
- orange zest, to garnish
- coriander seeds, to garnish

One of my favorite dishes to serve at a really special occasion is a big side of salmon. My whole family loves salmon so it checks all the boxes. This version is absolutely stunning and has a beautiful citrusy, slightly exotic, sweet flavor. And the color is gorgeous! Fit for any festive gathering or celebration. And it's actually very easy to make.

Place the salmon on a tray, skin-side down. In a bowl, combine the salt, sugar, coriander seeds, orange zest and grated beets. Mix well then pour the mixture over the salmon, making sure you have covered it evenly. Cover with plastic wrap or foil and refrigerate for 4–6 hours. You are not curing it, just using the beet mixture for the depth of flavor and color.

Preheat the oven to 425°F (220°C). Line a baking sheet with parchment paper.

In a small saucepan over medium heat, cook the maple syrup until slightly reduced, 5–6 minutes.

Scrape the beet mixture off the salmon and rinse the fish quickly under cold running water to remove the salt. Pat dry and place on the lined pan. Drizzle with a little olive oil and then brush with the maple glaze.

Roast for 20–25 minutes, brushing periodically with extra maple glaze.

Serve on a bed of lettuce and garnish with orange zest, coriander seeds and grated beet.

Tip If you want to cure the salmon, tightly wrap in plastic wrap or foil and place a weight on top (a chopping board or something else that's heavy) and refrigerate for 24 hours or up to 3 days. Skip the baking process and serve thinly sliced on bruschetta or baguette.

Whole roast chicken with spicy gravy & vegetable pilau rice

Serves 4–6

1 tsp chile powder
2 tsp ground paprika
1 tsp ground cumin
1 tsp ground coriander
½ tsp ground cinnamon
¼ tsp ground nutmeg
1 tsp salt, plus extra as needed
1 tsp ground black pepper
¼ cup (60 ml) oil
2 tsp tomato paste
juice of ½ lemon
small handful of fresh cilantro
small handful of mint
small thumb of ginger, grated
1–2 green chiles
2–3 garlic cloves, crushed
2–3 whole cloves
2–3 green cardamom pods
1 small cinnamon stick
1 whole chicken (3 lb 5 oz/1.5 kg)

for the vegetable pilau rice
1½ cups (300 g) basmati rice
1 small green chile
small handful of fresh cilantro
1 tbsp oil
1 onion, finely sliced
½ tsp cumin seeds
1 small cinnamon stick
1–2 garlic cloves, crushed
1 tsp ground cumin
1 cup (140 g) frozen vegetables
 (I use carrots, corn, peas)
small handful cauliflower florets
1 small potato, diced
lemon wedges, chargrilled
handful of chopped fresh cilantro

Roast chicken with all the trimmings is one of my favorite comfort foods. Here I have given the classic roast dinner a spicy boost! The vegetable pilau rice is a lovely dish to have on its own or as an accompaniment to any meat dish—add whatever vegetables you want.

In a bowl, combine the ground spices, salt and pepper. Add the oil, tomato paste and lemon juice and mix together well.

In a blender, blend the herbs, ginger, green chile and garlic into a paste and add to the spice mix. Stir through the whole spices and rub the mixture all over the chicken. Marinate for at least 6 hours or overnight.

Bring the chicken out of the fridge about 20 minutes before roasting. Preheat the oven to 425°F (220°C).

Place the chicken and marinade in a large roasting pan. Cover with foil and cook for 30 minutes. Remove the foil and baste the chicken with the marinade and pan juices.

Cook for a further 30–40 minutes, uncovered, until the juices run clear and the chicken is cooked. The chicken should be slightly crispy but moist inside.

For the vegetable pilau rice: Soak the rice in water for 20–30 minutes. Drain, then wash the rice until the water runs clear. In a blender, blend the chile and cilantro. Boil 3 cups (700 ml) of water.

In a large pot, heat the oil over medium heat. Add the onion and cook until softened but still pale. Add the whole spices and cook for about a minute; then add the garlic, chile-cilantro mixture and ground cumin. Stir and cook for a further 2–3 minutes. Add the vegetables and stir, coating with the spices. Stir in the rice until combined. Add the just-boiled water and about 1½ teaspoons of salt, according to taste.

Bring to a boil and then turn the heat to its lowest setting, cover and cook for 15–20 minutes, until the water has been absorbed and the rice is plump and cooked through.

To serve, layer the cooked rice on a large platter, put the whole chicken on the rice and spoon any gravy on top. Serve with lemon wedges and a good sprinkle of cilantro.

Lamb biryani with all the layers & crunchy filo rosettes

Serves 8–10

for the curry
1¼ cups (300 ml) oil
5–6 small potatoes, peeled and halved
2 onions, sliced
2 in (5 cm) cinnamon stick
2–3 green cardamom pods
2–3 whole cloves
4–6 whole black peppercorns
1 tsp cumin seeds
3 tsp ground coriander
½ tsp ground turmeric
1 tsp ground cumin
1–2 tsp chile powder
2 tsp ground paprika
1½ tsp salt
ground black pepper
2¼ cups (600 ml) tomato passata or puréed tomatoes
2–3 garlic cloves, crushed
2 lb 4 oz (1 kg) lamb (or chicken), cut into bite-sized pieces
1 tbsp tomato paste
1 tbsp white vinegar

for the saffron rice
4 cups (800 g) basmati rice
1 tbsp oil
1 tbsp butter or ghee
8 cups (1.9 liters) just-boiled water
4 tsp salt
red and yellow food coloring
¼ tsp saffron
4 boiled eggs, halved lengthways
handful of chopped fresh cilantro

Ingredients continued overleaf . . .

This is my mom's recipe (her version uses chicken) and it is hands down one of the best biryanis! We all say that, right, about our mother's cooking? But seriously, nothing takes me back home more than eating this delicious dish with its fragrant layers of saffron rice, fried onions and flavorful curry. It's a beautiful dish to serve for a celebration. Traditionally, biryani is cooked in a pot and then sealed with dough to create steam, which is referred to as dum. Mom always just covered the pot with a tight-fitting lid. To really wow your guests, though, use filo roses to create a sort of seal and make the dish look spectacular. I have used this filo inspiration from a dessert I made. It has a very special place in my heart.

For the curry: Heat ¾ cup (180 ml) of the oil in a small frying pan and fry the potatoes until golden, about 10 minutes.

In a large pot, heat the remaining ½ cup (120 ml) of the oil and fry the onions until golden. Using a slotted spoon, transfer to paper towels to drain. Set aside.

Add the whole spices to the same oil and fry for 1 minute, then add the ground spices, salt and pepper, tomato passata and garlic, and cook over low heat for 6–8 minutes. Add the lamb pieces and cook, covered, for a further 10 minutes.

Add the tomato paste, vinegar and fried potatoes to the pot and simmer until sauce clings to the meat, about 10 minutes. If it starts catching on the bottom, add a splash of water. The sauce should be a thick consistency and not too runny. Turn off the heat.

For the rice: Soak the rice in water for 20–30 minutes. Drain then wash the rice until the water runs clear.

In a large pot, heat the oil and butter, add the rice and stir until it just starts to become translucent, then add the just-boiled water and salt. Allow it to boil for 1–2 minutes, then turn the heat down to low and simmer, covered, for about 15 minutes until the water has been absorbed. The rice should be cooked, fluffy and separated.

Recipe continued overleaf . . .

ELABORATE DINNERS & FESTIVE FEASTS

for the filo rosettes
10–12 sheets store-bought filo pastry
11 tbsp (150 g) melted butter
oil or ghee, to drizzle
edible dried Persian rose petals to decorate (optional)

for serving
cucumber raita (see page 242)
tomato & onion kachumber (see page 242)

Mix about 1 cup of the cooked rice with a drop of red and yellow food coloring mixed with a little water. Soak the saffron in 1 tablespoon just-boiled water for a few minutes then stir into the colored rice and set aside.

Place a layer of curry into a large 8½-cup (2-liter) capacity ovenproof pot. Add a layer of cooked white rice to the pot, then a layer of the curry, and carry on until you have 3–4 layers, ending with rice.

Place the boiled eggs on top and then add your saffron rice, fried onions and chopped cilantro.

Preheat the oven to 350°F (180°C).

For the filo rosettes: Unroll the filo pastry and cover with a damp cloth. On a clean work surface, one at a time, place a pastry sheet with the long side towards you and brush with butter. Fold roughly accordion-style lengthways and then roll up to form a rosette. Repeat with remaining filo. Place each rosette on top of the biryani until the surface is fully covered.

Drizzle a little oil or ghee around the edges so it drips down the sides of the biryani.

Bake for 20–25 minutes or until the filo roses are golden.

Decorate with edible dried Persian rose petals, if desired. Serve hot with a cucumber raita and tomato and onion kachumber.

Tip This beautiful dish can also be made vegetarian by replacing the meat with 2 lb 4 oz (1 kg) of mixed mushrooms—portobello, shitake, white or brown button—or other vegetables of your choice.

You can skip the filo pastry. Instead, layer your biryani in a large pot with a tight-fitting lid. Put on the heat, drizzle ghee or oil down the sides of the rice in the pot, and cook, covered, on low heat for 15–20 minutes.

Mediterranean spiced lamb borek

Serves 6–8

for the filling
2 tbsp olive oil
1 onion, finely diced
2–3 garlic cloves, crushed
1 tsp salt
1 lb 5 oz (600 g) ground lamb
1½ tsp ground cumin
1 tsp ground coriander
1 tsp ground paprika
¾ tsp ground cinnamon
½ tsp chile flakes (optional)
ground black pepper
1 cup (240 ml) tomato passata or puréed tomatoes
¼ cup (60 ml) water
½ cup (85 g) finely chopped fresh apricots (raisin-sized pieces)
⅓ cup (35 g) pine nuts

for the filo
1 egg
2–3 tbsp yogurt
2–3 tbsp melted butter
12 sheets store-bought filo pastry
black and white sesame seeds (optional)
cucumber raita (see page 242), to serve

Crisp and rich, borek is a savory Turkish pastry. It's made by layering thin filo and various fillings. It can be made into cigar-shaped rolls or a pie. Traditionally served as breakfast in Turkey, it can really be served any time of the day. The fillings can be cheese, meat, greens or a mixture.

For the filling: In a large frying pan, heat the oil and fry the onion until softened—I like the onion to have a slight color to it. Add the garlic and salt. Add the lamb and fry until browned. Then add all the spices and pepper. Cook for a couple of minutes. Pour in the tomato passata and water then add the apricots and pine nuts. Turn the heat down and simmer for 20–25 minutes to reduce the liquid to a thick consistency. Once cooked, transfer to a shallow dish to cool completely.

Preheat the oven to 425°F (220°C).

For the filo: In a small bowl, whisk together the egg, yogurt and butter.

Unroll the filo pastry and cover with a damp cloth. Place parchment paper on your work surface and place a sheet of filo on it. Brush with the egg-yogurt wash (this prevents the filo from breaking). Place another sheet of filo on top and brush again with egg wash. Repeat until you have four layers.

Now place a third of the meat mixture along the longest edge, then roll up the filling and pastry into a log shape. Repeat until you have three logs, using all the filling.

Once you have three logs, still working on your parchment paper, starting from the middle, roll one log into a spiral. Join the three logs together, but not too tightly, and tuck them into the previous log if you can.

I like baking this in a 10 in (26 cm) cast-iron skillet, but you could also use a small baking dish. The spiral should fit snugly. Butter a skillet or dish and carefully slide the spiral off the parchment paper into the pan or dish. Brush the top with melted butter and sprinkle with sesame seeds (if using).

Bake until golden, 25–30 minutes. You can serve the borek hot or at room temperature, with cucumber raita alongside.

Chicken tagine with apricots served with couscous

Serves 4–6

for the marinade
2 tsp ground paprika
1 tsp ground turmeric
1 tsp ground cumin
1 tsp ground ginger
½ tsp ground cinnamon
1 tsp salt
ground black pepper
2–3 tbsp olive oil

for the tagine
8 bone-in chicken thighs
2 cups (500 ml) chicken stock
¾ cup (100 g) dried apricots
¾–1 in (2–3 cm) cinnamon stick
1 tbsp honey
¼ cup (60 ml) olive oil
2 onions, finely sliced
4–6 garlic cloves, crushed
14 oz (400 g) can chopped tomatoes
1 tbsp tomato paste

to serve
1½ cups (260 g) couscous, cooked
slivered almonds
pomegranate seeds
chopped fresh cilantro

This North African dish is inspired by our trip to Marrakesh a few years ago. Often seen being cooked outside in a tagine (a traditional North African clay pot), this dish is rich with depth of flavor and it is perfect for a special occasion. With divine spices and sweetness from the honey and apricots, it's a perfect Maghrebi dish to share with loved ones.

In a bowl, combine the marinade ingredients, then coat the chicken pieces in the mixture. Cover and chill overnight if you can, or for at least a couple of hours.

Heat the stock in a large pot. Place the apricots, cinnamon stick and honey in a bowl and just cover with a little of the hot stock. Set aside to soak.

Heat the olive oil in a large pot and fry the chicken until brown all over. Remove from the pot and set aside.

In the same oil, fry the onions until golden, then add the garlic. Stir in the tomatoes, tomato paste and apricots, including the soaking liquid.

Add the chicken pieces back to the pot, along with the remaining stock, and simmer over low heat until the chicken is cooked through and the sauce has thickened slightly, 20–25 minutes.

Serve with couscous and sprinkle with almonds, pomegranate seeds and chopped fresh cilantro.

Slow-cooked leg of lamb on pomegranate & rose rice

Serves 8–10

3¼–4½ lb (1.5–2 kg) leg of lamb
1 tsp salt
2–3 garlic cloves, crushed
1 tsp grated fresh ginger
juice of 1 lemon
4–5 tbsp olive oil
1 tsp ground cumin
1 tsp chile powder
2 tsp ground paprika
1 tsp ground coriander
3–4 whole cloves
3–4 green cardamom pods, seeds removed and crushed

for the pomegranate & rose rice
1–2 tbsp oil
1 large onion, finely sliced
2 cups (320 g) cooked basmati rice (made from about 1 cup/200 g dried rice)
pink food coloring (optional)
1 tsp rose water
2 tbsp pomegranate seeds
½ cup (8 g) chopped fresh cilantro
pesticide-free fresh rose petals (optional)

This is one of my favorite ways to roast a leg of lamb and it's perfect for a large gathering. It adds a lovely Indian twist to the traditional Western roast dinner. By slow-cooking the lamb (just the way I like it), the meat falls away from the bone and melts in your mouth. It's also bursting with the spicy flavors of cloves, cardamom and cumin. Served with my pomegranate and rose rice, this is a stunner of a dish that will leave your guests wanting more.

Place the lamb on a roasting pan. Prick with a fork and also make small cuts all over with a sharp knife.

In a small bowl, mix together the salt, garlic, ginger, lemon juice, oil and spices. Rub spice mix all over the lamb. Cover with foil and leave to marinate in the fridge overnight.

Next day, bring the lamb back to room temperature. Preheat the oven to 350°F (180°C).

Tightly wrap the lamb in a couple of sheets of foil, making sure there are no gaps for any steam to escape. Roast in the oven for 3.5–4 hours, until the lamb is tender and falls off the bone. Alternatively, you can cook for 2.5 hours, remove the foil and cook for a further 30 minutes to brown the top. Rest for 10 minutes

For the rice: Start 30–40 minutes before the lamb is cooked. Heat the oil in a small frying pan and fry the onion until golden and caramelized. Set aside on paper towels.

Arrange the cooked rice on a large platter. If you want colored rice, mix together some food coloring with the rose water in a small bowl. Stir in about 4 tablespoons of the cooked rice until colored, then scatter it over the plain rice. Top with the caramelized onions and pomegranate seeds.

Once the lamb has rested, place it on top of the rice and scatter with cilantro and rose petals (if using).

Machi fry with fried onions & naan

Serves 4

2–3 firm white fish fillets (like cod, halibut or snapper), about 1 lb 2 oz/500 g in total
2–3 tbsp oil
2 onions, sliced
generous 1 cup (300 g) tomato passata or puréed tomatoes
2 tsp ground coriander
1 tsp ground paprika
1 tsp chile powder
½ tsp ground cumin
½ tsp ground turmeric
1 garlic clove, crushed
½ tsp salt
ground black pepper
handful of chopped fresh cilantro
naan (see page 241)

This was one of the dishes Mom used to serve when we were kids when we went to the lake for vacations. With an abundance of fresh fish, it was enjoyed with hot roti. You could serve this as part of a feast, or as a weeknight meal. I like to serve this with my easy naan (see page 241). You could serve it with rice, too, although it's more of a dry curry.

Cut each fish fillet into 4 pieces.

In a large wok or frying pan, heat the oil over medium heat. Add the onions and fry until golden (being careful not to burn them). Remove and set aside on a paper towel.

In the same oil, fry the fish, in batches, until golden, then set aside on paper towels.

Add the tomato passata to the same pan, then stir in all the spices, garlic, salt and pepper and cook until the oil and tomatoes start to separate, about 15 minutes.

Gently place the fish in the pan and cover in the sauce, making sure you don't break them. Cook for a further 5–10 minutes to ensure the fish is coated in the sauce.

To serve, place on a serving dish and scatter with the fried onions and fresh cilantro. Serve with naan.

Lamb parsi in spicy gravy with lemon rice

Serves 4–6

for the lamb
- scant ½–⅔ cup (100–150 ml) neutral oil, for frying
- 1 in (3 cm) cinnamon stick
- 1–2 bay leaves
- 1–2 whole cloves
- 2 red onions, finely sliced
- 2 lb 4 oz (1 kg) boneless lamb, cut into bite-sized chunks
- 2–3 garlic cloves, crushed
- thumb-size piece of ginger, grated
- 2 tsp Kashmiri chile powder
- 1 tsp ground paprika
- 1 tsp ground turmeric
- 2 tsp salt
- 14 oz (400 g) chopped tomatoes (canned or fresh)
- 3 tbsp jaggery (or brown sugar)
- 2¾ tbsp white vinegar
- 1 tsp garam masala

for the lemon rice
- 2½ cups (500 g) basmati rice
- 1 tbsp butter
- 1 tbsp olive oil
- 1 onion, finely sliced
- 5 cups (1.2 liters) just-boiled water
- 2 tsp salt
- zest and juice of 1 lemon
- handful of chopped fresh cilantro

for serving
- roti or naan (see page 241)

A delicious curry with a wonderful sauce and a few key spices that work beautifully with lamb. It's perfect served with rice and naan or roti. My easy lemon rice adds a lovely citrusy note.

For the lamb: Heat the oil in a large pot over medium heat, then add the whole spices and stir for about a minute. Next, add the onions and cook gently until soft and caramelized. Add the lamb, garlic and ginger and continue cooking for a few minutes.

Next add the chile powder, paprika, turmeric and salt and cook for a further 3–4 minutes.

Stir in the chopped tomatoes and cook over low heat until the oil separates from the tomatoes—this an important stage and not to be rushed. Add a splash of water if the meat starts sticking to the pot, but not too much as it's a "dry" curry.

Pour in enough water to cover the lamb (a scant 1 cup/200 ml should do it). Cover with the lid and simmer over low heat for 1½ hours, or until the lamb is tender. Top up with a little more water if needed.

When the lamb is cooked and tender, add the jaggery, vinegar and garam masala and cook for a further 10–15 minutes.

For the lemon rice: Soak the rice in water for 20–30 minutes. Drain then wash the rice until the water runs clear.

Heat the butter and oil in a heavy-based pot with a lid. Add the onion and cook until pale golden.

Add the drained, washed rice, stirring with a wooden spoon until it starts to look translucent and sticks to the pot, 3–4 minutes.

Add the just-boiled water, then the salt and the lemon zest and juice. Bring to a boil, then reduce heat to the lowest setting and cover. Cook for 15–20 minutes until all the water has evaporated. Make sure that the heat is really low or the rice will stick to the bottom of the pot and burn. The rice should be fluffy, and the grains separate, not sticking together. Mix in the chopped cilantro.

Serve the lamb and gravy in a large dish with rice alongside so everyone can help themselves. You can also serve it with roti or naan.

North African chicken bastilla pie

Serves 6–8

½ cup (60 g) mixed nuts (I use sliced almonds and pine nuts)
10 tbsp (140 g) butter
3 tbsp olive oil, plus a little extra if needed
2 onions, finely sliced
¼ tsp salt
ground black pepper
1 lb 2 oz (500 g) boneless chicken thighs or breast
½ tsp ground cinnamon
½ tsp ras-el-hanout
½ tsp ground coriander
½ tsp ground cumin
¼ tsp garlic powder
½ tsp confectioners' sugar, sifted
6 eggs
14 oz (400 g) store-bought filo pastry

for serving
2 tbsp confectioners' sugar, sifted
2 tbsp ground cinnamon

This recipe was given to me by my younger sister Nish. It's full of North African flavors, which is part of her husband Sofiane's French Algerian heritage. It's a beautiful mixture of sweet and savory.

Toast the mixed nuts in a large frying pan over medium heat—keep any eye on them as they can burn easily. Remove from the pan, roughly chop and set aside.

In the same pan, heat 2 tablespoons of the butter and 2 tablespoons of the olive oil and fry the onions until caramelized. Remove from the pan and set aside.

Half-fill a pot with water and season with salt and pepper. Add the chicken and bring to a boil, then lower the heat and simmer until cooked and tender, 20–25 minutes.

Shred the chicken with a couple of forks and fry in the same frying pan as the onions (with a little more olive oil, if needed) over medium heat. Add the spices and the confectioners' sugar and cook until everything comes together, 5–7 minutes. Remove from the pan and set aside. Wipe out the pan.

Whisk the eggs in a bowl and season with salt and pepper. Add 1 tablespoon of the butter and 1 tablespoon of the olive oil to the pan and scramble the eggs. Once cooked, set aside.

Now for the assembling. You will need a round pie dish, or you can use a 9 in (24 cm) springform cake pan.

Preheat the oven to 350°F (180°C). Melt the remaining 7 tablespoons (100 g) butter. Brush a couple of sheets of filo with the melted butter and use to line the dish, butter-side up—I usually place them in different directions. Layer in one third of the chicken, scrambled eggs, onion, and nuts. Place another two sheets of filo on top, brush with butter and layer with another third of the ingredients. Repeat once more so you end up with three layers. Fold the edges of the pastry towards the middle of the pie, brush with butter, and then cover the top with ruffled pastry sheets and again brush with butter.

Bake for 25–30 minutes until golden. Leave to cool and then dust with sifted cinnamon and confectioners' sugar and serve.

ELABORATE DINNERS & FESTIVE FEASTS

Zucchini & goat cheese rosettes

Makes 10 rosettes

2 sheets store-bought puff pastry, thawed
2 zucchinis, cut lengthways and thinly sliced (use a mandolin if you have one)
3½ oz (100 g) soft goat cheese, crumbled, plus extra to garnish
¼ cup (25 g) grated Parmesan
salt and ground black pepper
1 egg, beaten
zest of 1 lemon, to garnish
tamarind chutney (see page 242) or chutney of your choice, to serve

This special dish was inspired by my favorite rose apple pie recipe. This version makes for the perfect side dish with any main meal and is ideal as a light lunch with a zesty salad.

Preheat the oven to 375°F (190°C). Grease and chill a 12-hole muffin pan.

Cut each sheet of pastry into roughly 1½ in (4 cm) wide strips (you should get 5 from each sheet).

Arrange the zucchini slices lengthways along the top of the long edge of the strip, making sure they overlap each other. Sprinkle with the goat cheese, Parmesan and salt and pepper. Fold the bottom half of the pastry up to encase the slices.

Working with one strip at a time, and starting from one end, roll up the enclosed zucchinis to form a rose. Place each rose in the prepared muffin pan. Brush with beaten egg.

Bake for 35–40 minutes or until the pastry is cooked. If needed, cover the top with foil to prevent the zucchinis burning.

Garnish with extra goat cheese and lemon zest. Serve hot as a light lunch with a salad and a sweet chutney.

Tip You can easily double this recipe. A combination of green zucchinis and yellow summer squash look really lovely, too.

This chapter is all about sharing—small bites you can enjoy with family and friends over drinks in the evening. Whether it's a celebration party or just a weekend gathering of friends, these light bites are perfect for the mezze or tapas style of eating. Equally, you could choose a favorite to have as an appetizer, if you're thinking of creating your own dinner menu from the book. From bhajias and chutneys to sparkling drinks, this chapter will be the entertainer's best friend. Your friends will love you even more!

Sunset snacks & sharing plates

Parmesan-crumbed paneer with chile & mayo

Serves 6–8 as an appetizer

2 blocks paneer cheese
  (18 oz/500 g in total)
1 cup (50 g) panko breadcrumbs
½ cup (50 g) grated Parmesan
salt and ground black pepper
1 egg, beaten
neutral oil, for frying
½ cup (115 g) mayonnaise
1–2 tbsp Thai sweet chile sauce
chile flakes

Paneer is quite a bland source of protein, which is usually dressed up with a spicy curry sauce. Using Parmesan in the crumbs gives a lovely, strong, nutty flavor that works well with paneer. This is the perfect addition to a mezze spread or finger food platter. Serve with a chile and mayo dipping sauce, or any other sauce that takes your fancy.

Cut the paneer lengthways into sticks about ¾ in (2 cm) thick.

In a bowl, mix together the breadcrumbs, Parmesan, salt and pepper.

Dip each paneer stick into the beaten egg, then coat in the crumb mixture. Set aside.

Heat a frying pan with just enough oil to cover the base. Shallow-fry the paneer sticks, in batches if needed, until golden all over, turning them with tongs.

To make the dipping sauce, simply mix the mayonnaise with chile sauce in a small bowl.

Once all of the paneer sticks are fried, place them on a platter with the chile dipping sauce on the side. Sprinkle them with chile flakes and extra salt, and serve.

Potato bhajias with cilantro chutney

Serves 8–10 as an appetizer

2 lb 4 oz (1 kg) medium-sized potatoes
ice-cold water
5¼ cups (450 g) chickpea (gram) flour
heaped ¾ cup (100 g) all-purpose flour
1½ tsp salt
1 tsp garlic powder
½ tsp chile powder
½ tsp ground turmeric
½ tsp citric acid
¼ tsp baking powder
handful of chopped fresh cilantro (optional)
2½ cups (600 ml) water
neutral oil, for deep-frying

for the cilantro chutney
bunch of fresh cilantro, stalks removed
2–3 green chiles
2 tbsp lemon juice
small handful of mint leaves
a little sugar, to taste
salt and ground black pepper

A much-loved snack, bhajias (also known as bhajis) are perfect as an appetizer or as a nibble with drinks when you're entertaining. Traditionally, however, bhajias are served to guests at cha pani, which is afternoon tea, along with samosas and various chutneys. Like vegetable fritters, bhajias can be made with different vegetables, bound with chickpea (gram) flour.

For the bhajias: Thinly slice the potatoes and set aside in ice-cold water.

In a large bowl, combine the chickpea flour, all-purpose flour, salt, spices, citric acid, baking powder, and the chopped cilantro. Slowly add the measured water, just until you have a batter thick enough to coat the back of a spoon—you may not need all of the water. Set the batter aside to rest for 20–30 minutes.

Heat the oil in a large wok or frying pan over medium–high heat. To check if the oil is hot enough, add a small piece of bread—if it turns golden, the oil is ready.

Drain and dry the potatoes, then dip the slices, one at a time, in the batter. Carefully place in the hot oil and fry until golden and cooked, turning to cook evenly. Don't worry if the shape is distorted, it adds to the rustic charm. Drain on paper towels.

For the cilantro chutney: Blend all the ingredients into a paste, adding more or less seasoning to taste. It can be stored for 3–4 days in the fridge.

Serve potato bhajias hot, with cilantro chutney on the side.

Spinach fritters

Serves 4-6 as an appetizer

generous 2 cups (180 g) chickpea (gram) flour
scant ½ cup (50 g) rice flour
1¼ tsp garlic powder
½ tsp Kashmiri chile powder
¼ tsp ground turmeric
¾ tsp salt
small handful of chopped fresh cilantro
2 tbsp lemon juice
2 tsp oil
1¼ cups (300 ml) cold water
neutral oil, for frying (I use sunflower)
7 oz (200 g) baby spinach leaves, washed and dried
dipping sauce or chutney, to serve

These nutritious fritters will surprise and delight. They are crispy and crunchy and, dipped in your favorite chutney, make a great evening snack to share with friends over drinks.

Place the flours, spices and salt in a bowl and mix. Stir in the chopped cilantro. Next add the lemon juice and oil and then the cold water. Mix to batter consistency.

Heat oil for frying (about 2½ in/6 cm deep) in a wok or large pot. To check if the oil is hot enough, add a small piece of bread—if it turns golden, the oil is ready.

Dip each spinach leaf into the batter then fry in the hot oil—don't crowd the pan. Turn the spinach leaves until they are golden all over. Lift out with a slotted spoon.

Place the fritters on a tray lined with paper towels to drain the excess oil. Once you have fried them all, serve straight away with a dipping sauce or your favorite chutney.

Tip Another way to serve these is to place the spinach fritters on a large serving platter, dollop with some yogurt and drizzle with a chile sauce or tamarind sauce. Garnish with finely diced red onion and tomato and a sprinkle of cilantro. Again, serve straight away.

Spiced hot-smoked salmon served with homemade crackers

Serves 10–12 as an appetizer

for the salmon
2 lb 4 oz (1 kg) fresh boneless salmon fillet, skin on
½ cup (100 g) brown sugar
¼ cup (70 g) salt
1 tsp chile flakes
ground black pepper

for the crackers
½ cup (70 g) pumpkin seeds
¼ cup (35 g) flaxseeds
¼ cup (35 g) sesame seeds
1 tsp sea salt, plus extra to sprinkle
1 cup (120 g) all-purpose flour
½ cup (120 ml) water
⅓ cup (80 ml) olive oil (or extra virgin olive oil if you prefer)

This is a great way to serve smoked salmon. Paired with homemade crackers, it's the perfect appetizer to start the weekend. You can buy hot-smoked salmon at the store, or if you have a smoker, you can do it yourself. This recipe is how my husband smokes his fish—usually without the chile, that's my addition!

For the salmon: Clean the salmon and pat it dry. Lay it on a baking sheet. Mix the sugar, salt, chile and pepper in a bowl and rub all over the salmon. Cover with foil and leave in the fridge overnight.

The next day, set up your smoker. Layer the base with your choice of sawdust, we tend to use mānuka. Place the salmon on the smoker rack and close the lid. Fill the smoker cups with methylated spirits and light. Ensure the smoker is on a heat- and flame-resistant surface, like concrete. Place the smoker box on the base and leave until the cups have burned out. Leave to cool a little. Open the lid and remove the salmon.

For the crackers: Preheat the oven to 350°F (180°C).

Put all the seeds, salt and flour in a large bowl and mix to combine. Add the water and oil and mix to form a dough. Divide the dough in half and roll each half between two sheets of parchment paper to ⅛ in (3–4 mm) thick.

Transfer to baking sheets and remove the top sheet of parchment paper. Sprinkle with extra sea salt.

Bake for 15–20 minutes or until lightly golden. Cool on wire racks and then break into chunks. They keep well in an airtight container for 1–2 weeks.

Serve the salmon at room temperature on a platter with the homemade crackers.

Pani puri with potato filling & tamarind & cilantro chutney

Makes 20–25

for the potato filling
3–4 medium potatoes, peeled and cubed
¼ tsp ground turmeric
⅓ cup (50–60 g) cooked or canned chickpeas (washed and drained)

for the pani
½ bunch of fresh cilantro
2–3 tbsp soft brown sugar or jaggery if you have it
small thumb of ginger, peeled and grated
2 green chiles, deseeded and finely chopped

for the puris
20–25 puris (see page 164)
cilantro garlic chutney (see page 26)
tamarind chutney (see page 242)
scant ½ cup (100 ml) plain yogurt
pomegranate seeds
fresh cilantro, torn
sev (fine Indian fried noodles) (optional)

Everyone loves these delicate little puris, which can be made at home (see page 164) or bought pre-made from your local Indian grocery store. Here, I have paired them with a wonderful savory potato filling, but the pastries are so versatile the possibilities are endless. They are a taste bomb of flavors meant to be eaten in one mouthful. I serve these all the time at my cooking classes as an appetizer and they're the perfect conversation starter.

For the potato filling: Boil the cubed potatoes in salted water with the turmeric until tender. Drain and leave to cool. Combine the potatoes with the chickpeas.

For the pani: Blend all the ingredients with ⅔ cup (150 ml) of water until smooth. Add another 3–7 tbsp (50–100 ml) of water and mix to make a runny sauce.

For the puris: Assemble the puris just before serving, so they remain crisp. Puris are very fragile, so carefully tap a small ¾ in (2 cm)-diameter hole in the top of each puri with the handle of a teaspoon. Place a small amount of the potato filling in the puri, drizzle over some cilantro garlic chutney, tamarind chutney and ½ teaspoon of yogurt and top with pomegranate seeds and cilantro to serve. Add the pani just before you are ready to eat one. You can sprinkle the puris with sev, if you wish.

These can get messy so be sure to have napkins on hand!

Tip You can assemble the puris just before your guests arrive or you can serve them on a large platter with all the ingredients so people can make their own. Jaggery and sev are available from any Indian supermarket.

Tuna & green chile croquettes

Makes 14

handful of chopped fresh cilantro
1–2 green chiles
3 cups (450 g) canned chunky-style tuna
5–6 potatoes, boiled and mashed
squeeze of lemon juice
salt and ground black pepper
1 egg, beaten
breadcrumbs, for coating
1 cup (240 ml) vegetable oil, for frying
dipping sauce or chutney, to serve

Using pantry ingredients, these croquettes are a simple way to impress family and friends. I love making them and they're a perfect appetizer or finger food for a party. Serve them with a dipping sauce of your choice—I like them with a sweet and spicy chutney.

In a blender, blend the cilantro and green chiles into a chunky paste.

In a large bowl, mix together the tuna, mashed potatoes, lemon juice and chile-cilantro paste, using a wooden spoon or by hand. Season to taste then mix again until thoroughly combined.

Divide the mixture into small sausage-like kebab shapes, about 3 in (8 cm) long and 1 in (3 cm) in diameter.

Dip the croquettes into the beaten egg and then coat with breadcrumbs.

Heat the vegetable oil in a shallow frying pan until hot. Fry the croquettes for about 6–8 minutes, turning to ensure an even color, until browned.

Remove from heat and drain on paper towels to remove any excess oil.

Serve with a dipping sauce of your choice.

Spicy shrimp with puri & yogurt

Serves 6–8 as an appetizer

for the shrimp
2 lb 4 oz (1 kg) raw shrimp, peeled and deveined
juice of 1 lemon
1 tsp salt
ground black pepper
1 tbsp oil
1 tsp chile powder
1 tsp ground paprika
5 tbsp (75 g) butter
3–4 garlic cloves, thinly sliced
½ tsp chile flakes
2 tbsp ketchup
plain yogurt, for serving
handful of chopped fresh cilantro

for the puris
2 cups (240 g) all-purpose flour, plus extra for dusting
½ tsp baking powder
½ tsp salt
2 tbsp oil
½–¾ cup (120–180 ml) cold water
neutral oil, for deep-frying

These are my mom's spicy chile shrimp, which she used to make on special occasions and served with chunky homemade fries and a salad. I've decided to change it up and serve the shrimp in puris as a sharing plate. Your guests can simply pick up a puri, add a spoonful of spicy shrimp, drizzle some yogurt over the top and enjoy.

For the shrimp: Wash and drain the shrimp, making sure you get rid of the excess water.

In a bowl, combine the lemon juice, salt, pepper, oil, chile powder and paprika. Gently stir the shrimp into the mixture, making sure they are well coated. Cover the bowl and refrigerate for 30–60 minutes to marinate. Meanwhile start on the puris.

For the puris: In a bowl, mix the flour, baking powder and salt with the oil. Slowly add the cold water, mixing until you have a soft dough. You may not need all the water.

Divide into 20–22 pieces and roll into balls. Sprinkle flour on your work surface and roll out each ball into rounds about 3–4 in (8–10 cm) in diameter.

Heat the oil in a deep medium-sized pot over medium heat. To check if the oil is hot enough, add a small piece of bread—if it turns golden, the oil is ready. Fry the puris in small batches until they are all cooked, 1–2 minutes on each side. Make sure to spoon hot oil over them as you are frying, as this will make the puris puff up, giving you the hollow inside. Place them on a plate lined with paper towels to soak up excess oil.

For the shrimp: When you are ready to cook the shrimp, drain off the excess liquid. Heat the butter in a frying pan over medium heat and add a splash of oil. Add the sliced garlic and cook until pale golden, then add chile flakes and the shrimp. Cook over low heat for 6–8 minutes.

Add the ketchup and cook for a further 2–3 minutes, or until the shrimp are cooked through. Make sure you don't overcook them as they will become chewy.

Once the shrimp are cooked, place a spoonful on each puri, with a dollop of yogurt and a sprinkle of cilantro.

Chicken pakoras in a curry leaf batter

Serves 4–6 as an appetizer

1 lb 2 oz (500 g) boneless chicken thighs, cut into bite-sized pieces
1 tsp crushed garlic
1 tsp minced ginger
1 green chile, finely chopped
1 tsp ground coriander
1 tsp ground cumin
½ tsp red chile flakes
handful of fresh curry leaves
heaped 1 cup (100 g) chickpea (gram) flour
1 tbsp cornstarch
½ tsp salt
¼ tsp baking soda
¾ cup (180 ml) water
neutral oil, for deep-frying
Thai sweet chile sauce, to serve

Pakoras are spiced fritters—also known as bhajis or bhajias in different Indian languages—usually made with vegetables dipped in a batter made from chickpea (gram) flour. You can use this recipe as a base to make different types of pakoras. It would also work well with cauliflower, eggplant, potatoes or onions.

Place the chicken pieces in a bowl and add the garlic, ginger, chile and spices. Stir to coat well then cover and refrigerate for 30–40 minutes to marinate.

Fry curry leaves in a little oil until crispy.

In a bowl, combine the flour, cornstarch, salt and baking soda. Crush in the curry leaves and mix. Add this mixture to the chicken and stir to coat the chicken.

Next, gradually add the water, mixing until you get a batter resembling thick cream—you may or may not need all off the water.

Heat the oil in a large pot over medium heat; it should come halfway up the wall of the pot to a 3–4 in (8–10 cm) depth. To check if the oil is hot enough, add a drop of batter—if it turns golden, the oil is ready. Once the oil is hot, start adding the chicken pieces in small batches. Fry for 6–8 minutes, turning them so they are cooked through and golden all over.

Once all the chicken is fried, serve it with Thai sweet chile sauce.

Cumin puri with mango chutney

Serves 4–6 as an appetizer

2 cups (240 g) all-purpose flour, plus extra for rolling
pinch of salt
½ tsp baking powder
1½ tsp cumin seeds
4 tbsp (60 g) ghee or butter, plus extra, melted, for brushing
few drops of lemon juice
⅔ cup (150 ml) hot water, plus extra if neeeded
cornstarch, for sprinkling
neutral oil, for frying
mango chutney (see page 60)

This is a deep-fried, homemade cracker that we used to have as kids. It makes a great afternoon treat on a weekend or shared with impromptu guests. I love this as part of a cheeseboard served with my delicious mango chutney (see page 60).

In a bowl, mix the flour, salt and baking powder. Add the cumin seeds. Rub in the ghee until the mixture resembles breadcrumbs. Add a few drops of lemon juice to the water and pour it into the flour. Mix to a soft dough. Cover and set aside for 30 minutes.

Divide the dough into 6 portions and roll each into a ball. Sprinkle flour on your work surface and roll out each ball into a large thin roti (circle).

Brush 3 rotis with melted ghee and sprinkle with cornstarch. Place another roti on top of each one to make two layers. Brush the top rotis with some ghee and sprinkle with a little cornstarch.

Roll up each pile of layered rotis to make a Swiss roll shape. Cut diagonally into 12–14 x ½ in (1 cm)-thick slices, slightly flattening each at an angle to show the layers. Lightly roll each slice with a rolling pin to flatten just a little.

Heat the oil (about 2 in/5 cm) deep) in a wok or large pot. To check if the oil is hot enough, add a small piece of bread—if it turns golden, the oil is ready. Fry the puri until golden and crisp on both sides. Remove from the pan and drain on paper towels.

Serve the puri with mango chutney.

Kesra bread with whipped feta & sumac-roasted chickpeas

Serves 4–6 as an appetizer

for the kesra bread
2 cups (325 g) fine semolina flour
¼ tsp salt
1 tbsp oil
scant ½ cup (100 ml) water
butter for cooking

for the chickpeas
14 oz (400 g) can chickpeas, drained and dried
2 tbsp olive oil, plus extra for drizzling
1 tsp sumac, plus extra for sprinkling
½ tsp chile flakes
½ tsp ground cumin
½ tsp salt
handful of chopped fresh cilantro

for the whipped feta
7 oz (200 g) feta
scant ½ cup (100 g) Greek yogurt
1 garlic clove, crushed
zest of ½ lemon

This is an Algerian semolina bread that I first tried with my sister Nish. Her husband, Sofiane, is French Algerian, and they both cook delicious Maghreb-inspired dishes. This is a lovely, easy flatbread that can be eaten any time of the day. I have paired it here with whipped feta and chickpeas to make a divine sharing plate.

For the kesra bread: Place the semolina flour in a large bowl and rub salt and oil into it until the texture resembles wet sand.

Add water slowly and knead the dough until soft. Rest for 30 minutes.

Divide the dough into 6 pieces and pat each into a rough circle 3–4 in (8–10 cm) in diameter (or you can use a rolling pin if you prefer). Using a fork, prick holes all over the circle.

Heat a nonstick frying pan over medium heat and add a little butter. Cook the bread until golden and crispy on both sides, 5–7 minutes in total. Cut each bread into quarters and then halve each quarter so you have eight triangles.

For the chickpeas: Preheat the oven to 400°F (200°C). Place the chickpeas on a baking sheet with the olive oil, spices and salt. Mix together well. Roast for 20–25 minutes until crispy.

For the whipped feta: In a food processor or blender, whip together all the ingredients until smooth and creamy.

To serve, swirl the whipped feta on a dish, drizzle with a little olive oil, add the roasted chickpeas and chopped cilantro and sprinkle over extra sumac. Serve with pieces of kesra bread as a scrumptious dip for your gathering.

Cassava fries with chile & lime

Serves 4–6 as an appetizer

3–4 large pieces fresh or frozen cassava (yuca)
1 cup (240 ml) neutral oil, for frying
2 eggs, lightly beaten
salt and ground black pepper
chile powder
lime or lemon wedges, to serve

These fries are so delicious and remind me of my childhood in Malawi. We would eat them sprinkled with lots of chile powder and salt and a squeeze of lime or lemon. Cassava or yuca, is known in some East African countries as mogo. It has an earthy, nutty flavor and is a starchy root vegetable. You can get it fresh in Pacific, South Asian, and Latin American supermarkets; it also comes frozen and peeled. I think this is the best way to eat it.

Place the cassava in a pot of boiling water and cook until a knife goes in easily, about 20 minutes.

Drain, cool and remove the woody core from the middle, then cut into similar-sized chunky fries.

Heat the oil in a large wok or frying pan over medium–high heat. To check if the oil is hot enough, add a small piece of bread—if it turns golden, the oil is ready.

Season the eggs with salt and pepper in a shallow bowl. Dip each fry into the egg, rotating to thoroughly coat the fry.

Fry the coated cassava fries in hot oil until golden and cooked through (you may need to work in batches). Drain on paper towels.

Season to taste with salt and chile powder. Serve with lime or lemon wedges for squeezing.

Ginger & lime sharbat

Makes about 2½ cups (600 ml) syrup

1½ cups (300 g) sugar
1½ cups (350 ml) just-boiled water
2 green cardamom pods, slightly crushed
1½ tbsp chopped fresh ginger
½ cup (120 ml) freshly squeezed lime juice, or more to taste
zest of 2 limes
small handful of mint leaves, finely chopped

for serving
ice
soda water or tonic water
sprig of mint

Growing up in Malawi, there was always a pitcher of sharbat in the fridge. Sharbat is a concentrated syrup made from fruit juice, water, sugar, spices and sometimes floral extracts. This recipe is a heavenly blend of ginger and lime that makes a deliciously refreshing drink. The syrup keeps in the fridge for three or four days.

In a heatproof jug, dissolve the sugar in the just-boiled water.

Add the cardamom and ginger and leave to cool. Once cooled, pick out the cardamom pods and discard, and then transfer the liquid to a blender. Add the lime juice and blend until smooth.

Pass the mixture through a sieve, then stir in the lime zest and mint. Refrigerate until required.

Serve chilled with ice, soda water or tonic water and a sprig of mint.

Raspberry & rose water limeade

Makes about 1½ cups (350 ml) syrup

3 cups (350 g) raspberries (fresh or frozen)
1 cup (200 g) sugar
scant ½ cup (100 ml) water
juice of 1 lime
2 tbsp rose water
non-alcoholic sparkling wine or soda water
ice
edible dried Persian rose petals
freeze-dried raspberries
mint leaves

Another delectable combination that makes a refreshing alternative to standard juice or soft-drink options. You can mix the syrup with alcohol if you wish.

Place the raspberries, sugar and water in a pot and bring slowly to a simmer for about 10 minutes. Add the lime juice and rose water and simmer for a further 5 minutes. Allow to stand for 30 minutes.

Strain the mixture through a sieve or cheeesecloth and return to the pot, then simmer again for 10 minutes or until slightly thicker.

Allow to cool completely before diluting with nonalcoholic sparkling wine or sparkling water and serving over ice. Decorate with edible dried Persian rose petals, freeze-dried raspberries and mint leaves.

Tip Traditionally used in black tea with cardamom, edible dried Persian rose petals are available online or in Middle Eastern and specialty food stores.

Hibiscus & star anise mocktail

Makes 4 glasses

2 hibiscus tea bags
2 cups (490 ml) water
1–2 star anise
3–4 thin slices fresh ginger
1 tbsp sugar
¼ cup (60 ml) lemon juice
hibiscus flowers in syrup
soda water (optional)
ice (optional)

Cool ocean breezes and hot days, that's what this refreshing mocktail reminds me of. It's a mouthwatering drink that will instantly transport you to a tropical beach. Hibiscus flowers are edible; they are also dried and made into tea.

Place the hibiscus tea bags in a small saucepan and add water. Bring to a boil, add star anise and simmer for 5 minutes. Squeeze the tea bags and strain the tea then place in the fridge to cool.

In a cocktail shaker (or if you don't have one, a mason jar will be fine), grind the ginger well with a muddler or pestle, then add the sugar and muddle together. Add the lemon juice and chilled hibiscus tea to the shaker or jar and shake well.

Strain the mocktail into glasses and place a hibiscus flower in each. You can also top with soda water and ice if you wish.

Tip I love to use the gorgeous hibiscus flowers in syrup that you can get in specialty stores.

Fried curry leaves & crumbed olives

Serves 4–6 as an appetizer

1 lb (470 g) jar extra-large pitted black or green olives
handful of curry leaves, plus extra for garnishing
neutral oil, for frying
1 cup (50 g) panko breadcrumbs
1 tsp garam masala
1 tsp Kashmiri chile powder
½ tsp chile flakes
salt and ground black pepper
½ cup (60 g) all-purpose flour
2 eggs, beaten

These are so good, you won't stop at one! Perfect for a gathering of family and friends for pre-dinner drinks. They are easy to make and bursting with flavor.

Drain the olives and dry them with paper towels.

Fry the curry leaves in a little oil until crispy and set aside.

Mix the breadcrumbs with all the spices, salt and pepper and crush the fried curry leaves into the mixture, setting a few aside for a garnish.

Place the flour, breadcrumb mixture, and beaten eggs in three separate bowls.

Add a few olives at a time to the flour, coating them well, then dip them in the egg, followed by the breadcrumb mixture. Set aside on a lined dish.

Once all the olives are coated, heat the oil (about 2 in/5 cm deep) in a large pot over medium heat. To check if the oil is hot enough, add a small piece of bread—if it turns golden, the oil is ready. Add the olives in batches and fry until golden. Remove with a slotted spoon and drain on paper towels.

Serve the olives in a bowl with extra fried curry leaves and toothpicks.

Tip You can buy Kashmiri chile powder at South Asian grocery stores. It is less spicy than red chile powder and gives a lovely color to a dish without too much heat.

Sugar, spice and all things nice, this chapter offers a selection of easy desserts and baking, using my signature style of combining East and West with a hint of spice to take it all to another level. Drawing inspiration from my family, you'll find French, Middle Eastern, Kiwi and Indian inspired sweet treats in the following pages. Every dish feels like a decadent treat; sumptuous, indulgent and guaranteed to make your guests feel extra special.

Sugar & spice

Strawberry Charlotte cake

Serves 8–10

for the syrup
⅔ cup (150 ml) water
2 tbsp sugar
juice of ½ lemon

for the cake
24–36 ladyfinger cookies (savoiardi)
14 oz (400 g) strawberries, washed and halved, plus extra to decorate the top
1 cup (250 g) mascarpone
⅓ cup (75 g) sugar
zest of 1 lemon
1 tsp vanilla extract
1 cup (250 ml) heavy cream, whipped
edible flowers, to decorate (optional)

This very retro, French-inspired dessert is light and fluffy and simple to make. It is traditionally made with Bavarian cream (a mix of egg yolks, milk and sugar), but I've used a cream and mascarpone filling. With fresh strawberries and softened ladyfinger cookies, it's a sure crowd-pleaser and perfect at a summer celebration.

For the syrup: Place the water in a saucepan and add the sugar and lemon juice. Bring to a boil and simmer until syrupy, about 10 minutes. Set aside.

For the cake: Cut ½ in (1 cm) off the end of each ladyfinger and dip the flat side in the syrup. Line the sides of an 8–9 in (20–22 cm) springform cake pan with the ladyfingers, standing vertically, dipped-side down. Line the base of the pan with dipped ladyfingers as well—you will have to cut the fingers to fit. Place half of the measured strawberries on top.

Beat the mascarpone, sugar, lemon zest and vanilla until smooth. Fold in the whipped cream and mix together. Spread half of the mixture over the strawberries. Repeat with another layer of syrup-dipped ladyfingers, the remaining strawberries and the rest of the cream mixture.

Refrigerate overnight, or for at least 4–6 hours. When ready to serve, remove the side of the pan. If you can easily slide the cake off the base, do so, but don't worry if you can't.

Decorate with a ribbon or twine, fresh strawberries and edible flowers, if desired.

Tip Ladyfingers are also known as savoiardi. I used jumbo ladyfingers for effect and doubled the recipe for the photo—but the recipe above uses traditional-sized ones.

Carrot halva spring rolls

Makes 12–14

5 cups (1.2 liters) milk
9 oz (250 g) carrots, peeled and grated
¼ tsp ground cardamom (optional)
5 tbsp (75 g) butter
scant 1 cup (175 g) sugar
¼ cup (40 g) raisins (optional)
12–14 spring roll wrappers
neutral oil, for frying (optional)
confectioners' sugar, for dusting
edible flowers, to garnish
mascarpone or ice cream

Carrot halva, or gajar halva as it's also known, is one of my favorite Indian sweets. It's caramelized, buttery and sweet and brings back fond memories of special occasions with family. I decided to add a twist to the traditional version, which you would usually eat out of a bowl, and encase the halva in pastry to make sweet spring rolls. The mascarpone is a must as it cuts into the sweetness and takes this dessert to a new level.

Place the milk, carrots and cardamom (if using) in a heavy-based pot and cook over high heat, stirring occasionally, until the liquid has evaporated, 25–30 minutes. Keep a close eye on it—you don't want it to catch on the bottom of the pot.

Add the butter, sugar and raisins (if using) and stir with a wooden spoon until the butter has melted and the sugar has dissolved.

Cook for a further 10–15 minutes, stirring frequently, until the mixture starts to leave the side of the pan. Mix and transfer to a shallow dish to cool, or chill in the fridge for 30 minutes.

Put a tablespoon of filling in the center of each spring roll sheet. Bring opposite corners to the middle and then roll up like a cigar—it needs to be nice and tight.

You can shallow-fry them until golden or bake them in the oven.

To shallow-fry, heat the oil (about 2 in/5 cm deep) in a pot over medium heat. To check if the oil is hot enough, add a small piece of bread—if it turns golden, the oil is ready. Add your spring rolls in batches and cook until golden all over, about 2 minutes each side. Set aside on paper towels.

To bake, preheat the oven to 350°F (180°C). Place spring rolls on an oiled baking sheet. Brush with a little oil or melted butter and bake for 20–25 minutes until golden.

Dust cooked spring rolls with confectioners' sugar, garnish with edible flowers and serve with mascarpone or ice cream.

Peach meringue cake

Serves 6–8

for the cake
7 tbsp (100 g) softened butter
½ cup (100 g) brown sugar
zest of 2 lemons
3 eggs
½ cup (60 g) all-purpose or
    gluten-free flour
½ cup (40 g) ground almonds
1½ tsp baking powder
2 tbsp lemon juice
2 fresh ripe peaches, pitted
    and quartered

for the meringue
3 egg whites
¾ cup (150 g) superfine sugar

for the caramelized peaches
3 tbsp sugar
1 tbsp butter
1 tbsp apple cider vinegar
½ tsp ground cinnamon
¼ tsp ground cardamom
2 fresh ripe peaches,
    pitted and quartered

crème fraîche or yogurt, to serve

I love using fruit in cakes—I'm not talking dried fruit cake here, but chunky bits of fresh fruit. The peach adds a lovely dimension to the cake. And the meringue just finishes it off— with a dollop of the caramelized peaches . . . just sublime.

Preheat the oven to 325°F (160°C). Line an 8 in (20 cm) springform cake pan with parchment paper.

For the cake: Cream the butter, brown sugar and lemon zest in the bowl of a stand mixer until pale and fluffy (alternatively, this can be done with a wooden spoon and a bowl).

Add the eggs one at a time, making sure they are fully incorporated between each addition. Stir in the flour, ground almonds, baking powder and lemon juice until smooth, taking care not to over-mix.

Pour the cake batter into the pan and arrange the peaches in the batter. Bake for 30 minutes until lightly golden. While the cake is baking, make the meringue.

For the meringue: Whisk the egg whites on high speed until they form peaks, then add the sugar 1 tablespoon at a time until the sugar has dissolved. Whisk until glossy and stiff.

Remove the cake from the oven when lightly golden and spread the meringue over the cake in swirly patterns.

Bake for a further 25–30 minutes or until the meringue is slightly colored.

For the caramelized peaches: While the cake is baking, place the sugar in a pot over low heat and gently swirl until it turns amber colored. Add the butter, vinegar and spices, and then the peaches. Cook over medium heat until the peaches are soft and golden, 5–7 minutes.

Remove the cake from the oven and set aside to cool for a few minutes. Run a knife around the edges before releasing the spring at the side of the cake pan. Spoon the caramelized peaches on the top and serve warm with crème fraîche or yogurt.

Tip You can use any stone fruit for this. Pears and apples also work well.

Rose & berry Paris–Brest

Serves 8–10

for the sugared rose petals
2 fresh pesticide-free roses
1 egg white, lightly beaten
1 small bowl superfine sugar

for the choux pastry
7 tbsp (100 g) butter
½ cup (120 ml) milk
½ cup (120 ml) water
1¼ cups (150 g) all-purpose flour
1 tsp confectioners' sugar
4 eggs, plus 1 extra, beaten, for brushing

for the cream filling
2 cups (480 ml) heavy cream
2 tsp confectioners' sugar
1 tbsp sour cream
scant 1 cup (150 g) fresh raspberries, plus extra for decorating
1 cup (150 g) fresh strawberries, sliced if you like

for the icing
1 tsp rose water
1–2 tsp just-boiled water
1 cup (115 g) confectioners' sugar

The Paris–Brest was a dessert created in 1910 to commemorate the Paris–Brest–Paris bicycle race. The shape represents a wheel of a bicycle, and my recipe is dedicated to my husband, who has been a keen triathlete and cyclist for many years.

For the sugared rose petals: Prepare these the night before. Remove each rose petal from the bud and rinse under water. Place on a wire rack and leave until completely dry. I use some of the leaves, too. Using a paintbrush, paint each petal with egg white. Lightly sprinkle with sugar to coat each petal and gently shake off any excess. Return to the wire rack to dry overnight.

For the choux pastry: Preheat the oven to 400°F (200°C). Line two baking sheets with parchment paper. Draw a 2½ in (6 cm) circle on each sheet and then flip the paper over.

Melt the butter with the milk and water in a saucepan over medium heat. Add the flour and confectioners' sugar, then beat with a wooden spoon until the mixture starts to come away from the sides. Let it cool and transfer to a stand mixer or mixing bowl.

Mix using the paddle attachment (or a handheld electric mixer), then add the 4 eggs, one at a time, mixing well after each addition. The mixture should be thick and glossy. Spoon the mixture into a pastry bag with a ¾ in (2 cm) round tip. Pipe one ring just inside the circle on the parchment paper and a second ring just inside the first; they should touch. Repeat on the second baking sheet. Brush the dough with the beaten egg.

Bake for 15 minutes, then reduce the oven temperature to 375°F (190°C) and bake for a further 30 minutes, or until puffed and golden. Turn off the oven and allow the pastry to cool in the oven, with the door ajar. Then transfer one pastry ring to a serving plate.

For the cream filling: Beat the cream, confectioners' sugar and sour cream together until soft peaks form. Pipe or spoon this onto the pastry ring on the plate, and then arrange the berries on top. Add more cream on top of the berries. Place the second pastry ring on top.

For the icing: Mix the rose water with 1 teaspoon of the just-boiled water. Mix in the confectioners' sugar, a little at a time, until smooth. It should be thick but spreadable (you can add the remaining teaspoon of hot water, if needed). Spread the icing on the top pastry. Decorate with the sugared rose petals and more berries.

Galette des rois

Serves 6

2 sheets store-bought butter puff pastry
1 whole almond (optional)
confectioners' sugar, to dust (optional)
mascarpone or whipped cream, to serve

for the glaze
1 egg yolk
1½ tsp heavy cream

for the almond cream filling
1 egg
⅓ cup (75 g) sugar
1¼ cups (100 g) ground almonds
1 tsp vanilla extract
3½ tbsp butter, at room temperature

A elegant yet easy recipe given to me by my sister Farha and her French Algerian pâtissier-chef husband, Wafi. They have a café-bakery in Abu Dhabi and the delights that come out of it are sensational. Traditionally, there is a "feve" (fava bean) hidden inside the almond cream, and whoever finds it is made king or queen for the day and wears a crown. I use a whole almond instead. A fun thing to do at a dinner party.

Preheat the oven to 350°F (180°C).

Cut an 8 in (20 cm) diameter circle out of one pastry sheet and a 9 in (22 cm) circle out of the other. Place in the fridge to firm up while you make the filling.

For the glaze: In a small bowl, whisk together the egg yolk and cream. Set aside.

For the almond cream filling: Whisk the egg and sugar together until light and fluffy. Add ground almonds, vanilla and butter and mix for a few minutes until smooth.

Spread the filling onto the 8 in (20 cm) pastry circle, leaving ¾ in (2 cm) free around the edge. Brush the edge with a little of the glaze. Press the whole almond (if using) into the filling.

Place the 9 in (22 cm) pastry circle on top and press gently around the edge to seal the pastry. You can use the blunt edge of a knife or a fork to seal it.

Brush with the glaze and then, starting from the center, score a spiral all around the pie. It makes a lovely design.

Bake for 45 minutes or until golden. Remove from the oven, leave to rest for a few minutes then dust with confectioners' sugar, if desired. Serve with mascarpone or whipped cream.

Mango & cardamom semifreddo with baked Alaska

Serves 4–6

for the semifreddo
1 cup (150 g) chopped fresh mango, or ½ cup (120 ml) canned mango pulp
2½ cups (600 ml) heavy cream
1¼ cups (300 ml) condensed milk
3–4 green cardamom pods, seeds extracted and crushed
chopped mango, chopped strawberries or whole raspberries (optional)

for the meringue
2 cups (400 g) superfine sugar
1 cup (240 ml) egg whites
pinch of salt
pinch of cream of tartar
dash of vanilla extract

I have always wanted to create a baked Alaska, so, inspired by the luscious versions on Instagram, I decided to make one with the mango ice cream from my first cookbook, *My Indian Kitchen*, but this time with a few additions. You'll need to make the semifreddo the day before you serve it.

For the semifreddo: In a blender, purée the chopped mango. (If you're using canned mango pulp, you can skip this step.)

In a large bowl, whisk the cream until it starts to thicken. Slowly whisk in the condensed milk. Add the mango purée or pulp and cardamom seeds and whisk until thick. At this stage add the chopped fruit or whole raspberries (if using) and mix through.

Line a 4¼-cup (1-liter) glass bowl with plastic wrap so it's hanging over the sides. Pour mixture into the bowl, cover with the plastic wrap and freeze (preferably overnight).

For the meringue: Half-fill a pot with water and bring to a simmer. Place the sugar and egg whites in a mixing bowl—use the bowl of a stand mixer, if you have one. Place the bowl over the simmering water (without touching the water). Stir with a spatula until the sugar dissolves, 6–8 minutes. To check, put a little of the mixture on a spoon, let cool briefly then rub between your thumb and forefinger—it shouldn't feel grainy. Once it feels smooth, add the salt.

Using a stand mixer or electric beater, whisk on a high speed until thick and glossy. Then add the cream of tartar and vanilla and whisk until stiff peaks form.

Remove the ice cream from the freezer, turn out onto a cake stand, and remove the plastic wrap. Cover the ice cream with a thick layer of meringue—you can go a little crazy with this, pull it into different directions to form spikes or you can use a pastry bag and create rosettes. Put it back in the freezer until you are ready to serve.

Just before serving, use a brûlée torch to brown the meringue and serve immediately, using a hot knife to slice.

Tip You can easily double the recipe to serve more. And use store-bought ice cream to save time. You can stir nuts, different fruit or chocolate chips into the ice cream, too.

Rose, raspberry & pistachio cream rolls

Makes 18–20

3–4 sheets store-bought puff pastry
neutral oil
3⅓ cups (800 ml) heavy cream
1 tsp ground cardamom
1 tsp rose water
1 cup (115 g) confectioners' sugar, for dusting
freeze-dried raspberries
¼ cup (20 g) ground pistachios
edible dried Persian rose petals

These pastry cream rolls are reminiscent of the cream horns my mom used to make for special occasions—usually birthdays—in Malawi. There were six of us (including our parents), so February, March, May, June and July were busy months for my mom! We always had birthday parties and, as twins, ours always felt so special. This is my version, they are quick and easy to make, but you do need a set of metal cannoli tubes on hand.

Preheat the oven to 350°F (180°C). Line two baking sheets with parchment paper.

Lay the puff pastry sheets on a floured surface. Cut into 1 in (2.5 cm) wide strips. You should have 18–20.

Lightly grease some metal cannoli tubes with oil and wrap a strip of pastry around the tube, making sure it overlaps slightly. Repeat until all the strips are used. Place the pastry tubes on the lined pans.

Bake for 20–25 minutes or until golden. Place on wire racks until completely cool. Remove the pastry rolls from the cannoli tubes.

Whisk the cream, cardamom and rose water until soft peaks form. Use a pastry bag (or plastic food bag with the end snipped off) to pipe the cream into the pastry rolls. Dust liberally with confectioners' sugar and decorate with freeze-dried raspberries, pistachios and rose petals.

Tip You can sweeten the cream with confectioners' sugar, if you like. Traditionally used in black tea with cardamom, dried Persian rose petals (used for tea) are available online or in Middle Eastern and specialty food stores.

Baklava cheesecake with orange blossom syrup

Serves 8–10

for the base
2 cups (250 g) pistachios
1⅓ cups (200 g) mixed nuts (almonds, walnuts, hazelnuts)
¼ cup (50 g) sugar
1 tsp ground cinnamon
½ tsp ground cardamom
12 sheets store-bought filo pastry
9 tbsp (125 g) butter, melted

for the filling
2 cups (450 g) cream cheese, at room temperature
⅔ cup (120 g) sugar
2 tbsp all-purpose flour
3 eggs
⅓ cup (75 ml) heavy cream

for the orange blossom syrup
½ cup (120 ml) honey
½ cup (120 ml) water
½ cup (100 g) sugar
2 tsp rose water
2 tsp orange blossom water
pinch of saffron (optional)

dried rose petals, fresh rose petals and extra pistachios, to garnish

Nothing beats the flavors of a gorgeous baklava—think orange, saffron, honey and pistachios. Imagine the perfection of combining those flavors with a creamy baked cheesecake. A Middle Eastern-inspired treat, perfect for a celebration. I like it with a cup of apple tea.

Preheat the oven to 350°F (180°C). Grease a 9 in (22 cm) springform cake pan.

For the base: Place the nuts in a food processor and pulse until finely chopped. Transfer to a large bowl, add the sugar and the spices and stir to combine.

Place a sheet of filo pastry in the base of the cake pan, with the ends hanging over the edge of the pan, and brush with melted butter. Cover with one more layer of filo brushed with butter. Sprinkle a layer of spiced nuts over the top. Butter 2 more filo sheets and place them on top of the first layer of pastry and nuts, rotating them so the sides of the pan are covered. Repeat the process with the remaining filo pastry and nut mixture, ending with a layer of filo.

For the filling: Using an electric mixer or stand mixer, whisk the cream cheese with the sugar until fluffy, about 2 minutes. Add the flour, eggs and heavy cream and whisk until just combined. Pour into the prepared filo base. Cut the overhanging filo around the edge of the cake pan.

For the syrup: In a saucepan, combine the honey, water and sugar over medium–high heat, stirring until the sugar dissolves. Cook until the syrup thickens, then remove from the heat. Add the rose water, orange blossom water and saffron (if using). Stir to combine and set aside.

Bake the cheesecake for 45 minutes, then carefully remove the sides of the cake pan and bake for a further 20–25 minutes until golden. Remove the cheesecake from the oven and pour the syrup over the edges and sides. Allow to cool completely, then garnish with dried rose petals, fresh rose petals and pistachios, and serve with a cup of apple tea.

Halva with scarlet poached pears

Serves 4-6

for the halva
- 1¼ cups (300 ml) heavy cream
- 2 cups (500 ml) milk
- ¼ cup sugar
- 1 tsp agar-agar, mixed with 1 tbsp water
- 2 tsp semolina
- 1 tsp vanilla extract

for the pears
- 2 cups (480 ml) non-alcoholic red wine
- 1 beet, peeled and sliced
- 1 tbsp sugar or maple syrup
- 2 tsp freshly squeezed lemon juice
- 1–1½ in (3–4 cm) cinnamon stick or 1 star anise
- 4 small firm-ripe pears, peeled, with stems on

Very similar to the Italian panna cotta, halva is a delicious, creamy Indian dessert that is easy to make and a lovely, cooling way to finish off your meal. Serve with the scarlet-colored pears and you will wow your guests. I love poaching pears as they go so well with creamy desserts.

For the halva: Whisk the cream and milk together with an electric mixer. Pour into a pot over medium heat, add the sugar and bring to a boil.

Reduce the heat and then add the agar-agar and water mixture, semolina and vanilla. Simmer for 6–8 minutes.

Pour into 4–6 shallow dessert bowls, or a shallow 4-cup (950 ml) serving dish, and allow to cool. Put it into the fridge while you make the pears.

For the pears: Select a deep pot large enough to hold the upright pears, and cut a circle of parchment paper slightly larger than the diameter of the pot.

Place all the ingredients (except the pears) in the pot and bring to a boil until the sugar dissolves.

Cut a thin slice off the bottom of each pear so it can stand upright. Place the pears in the pot and cover with the parchment paper, tucking the sides down to stop the steam escaping. Poach until the liquid is reduced and syrupy, about 25–30 minutes.

The pears can be chilled and brought to room temperature when ready to serve.

To serve, place a whole pear on each halva bowl. Alternatively, leaving the stem end intact, make about six slices into each pear. Fan out the pear over the halva.

Rhubarb & star anise crème brûlée

Serves 6

1 lb (450 g) rhubarb, chopped
¾ cup (150 g) sugar
2 whole star anise
2½ cups (600 ml) heavy cream
6 egg yolks
⅓ cup (70 g) sugar, plus extra for topping

These flavors are truly sensational! Inspired by the rhubarb and star anise ice cream I created, I knew I wanted to use this flavor combination again. It's perfect in crème brûlée—my favorite dessert.

Preheat the oven to 325°F (160°C).

In a pot, cook the rhubarb, sugar and 1 star anise over medium heat for about 10–12 minutes or until the sugar has dissolved. Discard the star anise; set the rhubarb aside to cool.

In another saucepan, heat the cream and the second star anise over medium heat for 5–6 minutes until almost boiling. Remove from the heat and set aside to allow the star anise to infuse.

Beat the egg yolks and sugar in a large bowl until pale—use an electric mixer if you have one, it will give the best results. Add the cream to the egg yolks, discarding the star anise, and stir until combined.

Select six ⅔-cup (150 ml) ramekins and spoon the rhubarb mixture into the base of each, then pour the cream mixture over the top. Alternatively, you can use a 4-cup (950 ml) dish—I do prefer individual crème brûlées, though.

Place the ramekins in a roasting pan and pour boiling water into the pan to come halfway up the sides of the ramekins.

Bake for 30–35 minutes until just set. Remove the ramekins from the oven and set aside to cool before refrigerating for 3–4 hours or overnight.

A little while before serving, sprinkle the top of each ramekin with sugar, making sure you cover the entire top. Using a brûlée torch or a hot broiler, brûlée the top until it caramelizes. I then put them back into the fridge until needed.

Tip You can make these the day before you need them.

Orange & rose almond cake

Serves 6–8

2 cups (170 g) ground almonds
½ cup (100 g) sugar
2 tsp baking soda
½ cup (120 g) plain Greek yogurt
¼ cup (60 ml) olive oil
3 eggs
zest and juice of 1 orange
1 tsp rose water
pinch of saffron mixed with a little water (optional)
confectioners' sugar, to dust
edible dried Persian roses, to serve

This is a beautiful cake to bake if you have to take something for a morning tea or to share with impromptu visitors. It's easy to put together and tastes great any time of day. I have used saffron in this recipe as it adds to the floral notes—however, you can leave it out if you don't have it.

Preheat the oven to 350°F (180°C). Grease and line an 8–9 in (20–22 cm) cake pan with parchment paper.

In a large bowl, mix together the ground almonds, sugar and baking soda.

Add the yogurt, oil, eggs, orange juice and zest, rose water, and saffron water, if using. Mix well. Pour into the prepared pan.

Bake for 50–55 minutes or until a skewer come out clean.

Cool, then remove from the pan and decorate with confectioners' sugar and Persian tea roses.

Tip Traditionally used in black tea with cardamom, edible dried Persian rose petals are available online or in Middle Eastern and specialty food stores.

Cinnamon plum clafoutis

Serves 4

1½ cups (350 ml) half and half
  (or 1 cup/240 ml milk and
  ½ cup/120 ml heavy cream)
3 eggs
2 tbsp melted butter
½ cup (100 g) sugar
½ cup (60 g) all-purpose flour
pinch of salt
¼ tsp ground ginger
¼ tsp ground cinnamon
12 oz (350 g) jar black Doris
  plums or 4–6 fresh plums,
  cut in half and pitted
confectioners' sugar, to dust
ice cream or whipped cream,
  to serve

This easy French dessert is a tender, milky, sponge-like cake baked around tart fruit. It's traditionally made with cherries, but you can actually use any fruit. You can even have it for breakfast! I have used canned black Doris plums, which work really well. I love warm desserts with fruit, and the ginger and cinnamon add another lovely warming touch.

Preheat the oven to 350°F (180°C). Butter a 9 in (23 cm) skillet or pie dish.

In a mixing bowl, whisk the half and half, eggs and butter together.

In a separate large mixing bowl, mix the sugar, flour, salt and spices.

Pour the wet ingredients into the dry ingredients and mix until you have a smooth batter.

Pour the batter into the prepared dish and arrange the plums (whole, if using canned) on top.

Bake for 30–35 minutes or until just set.

Dust with confectioners' sugar and serve warm with ice cream or whipped cream.

Gulab jamun

Makes 16

for the syrup
2 cups (400 g) sugar
4 cups (950 ml) water
4–6 drops rose water
pinch of saffron

for the gulab jamun
1 cup (100 g) powdered milk
2 tbsp self-rising flour
2 tsp fine semolina
2 tbsp ghee
4 tbsp milk
neutral oil, for frying
edible dried Persian rose petals, to garnish
mascarpone or whipped cream, to serve

This very popular Indian sweet, which translates as "rose plum," is actually fried dough balls soaked in a rose and saffron sweet syrup. A little like doughnuts, my non-Indian friends just love them, and I like to serve them with mascarpone or whipped cream.

For the syrup: Place the sugar in a large heavy-based pot with the water and stir over low heat until the sugar dissolves. Bring to a boil and add the rose water and saffron. Take off the heat and set aside to cool.

For the gulab jamun: Mix the powdered milk, flour, semolina and ghee in a bowl, and gradually add just enough of the milk to make a soft dough. Mix until smooth.

Using your hands, roll the dough into about 16 small balls.

Add enough oil to a deep pot or wok so it is about a third full and place over medium heat. To check if the oil is hot enough, add a small piece of bread—if it turns golden, the oil is ready.

Fry the balls until dark golden all over. Be careful as they get dark quite quickly. Use a slotted spoon to remove them from the hot oil and transfer them to the syrup pot.

When all the balls are fried and in the syrup, bring the syrup back to a boil, then remove from the heat. Cool the gulab jamun to room temperature, garnish with dried rose petals and serve with a dollop of mascarpone or whipped cream.

Pavlova crown with caramel & rose shards

Serves 10

for the pavlova
6 egg whites, at room temperature
½ tsp cream of tartar
1½ cups (300 g) superfine sugar
1 tsp cornstarch
1 tsp white vinegar
1 tsp vanilla extract
berries, pistachios and pomegranate seeds to decorate

for the rose cream
1¼ cups (300 ml) heavy cream
a couple of drops of rose water

for the caramel & rose shards
1 cup (200 g) sugar
¼ cup (60 ml) water
pinch of saffron (optional)
1 tsp salt flakes
1–2 tbsp edible dried Persian rose petals

An absolute must at any family gathering, this Kiwi classic has been given my signature twist. It looks sensational and is a favorite in our family. I first tried it when I spent Christmas with my husband's family for the first time, about 26 years ago. You can decorate it with anything you want, and if you don't want to make a crown, you can skip that process. It will be just as delicious.

Preheat the oven to 325°F (160°C). Draw an 8 in (20 cm) circle on parchment paper and place upside down on a baking sheet.

For the pavlova: Whisk the egg whites with an electric mixer on medium speed until stiff (a stand mixer is helpful if you have one). Add the cream of tartar, then gradually add sugar, a tablespoon at a time. Whisk for 10–12 minutes until the sugar is dissolved. To check this, stop the machine and rub some mixture between your thumb and forefinger; if it feels rough, continue whisking for up to 15 minutes total time.

Add the cornstarch, vinegar and vanilla. Turn the mixer to high for 40 seconds. The mixture should now be thick and glossy and should stay in whichever position you put it.

Using the circle as a guide, pile the mixture in a circular mound on the parchment paper, gently flattening the top and smoothing the edges. Then, using an offset spatula, make upward strokes to create a crown around the edges. You will need to press very lightly into the pavlova to create the shape.

Place it in the oven and immediately turn the oven down to 225°F (110°C) for 1 hour.

For the rose cream: Whisk the heavy cream with the rose water until soft peaks form, being careful not to over-mix.

For the caramel & rose shards: Line a baking sheet with foil. Place the sugar, water and saffron (if using) in a saucepan over low heat, stirring until the sugar has dissolved. Increase the heat to high and cook for 4–5 minutes, swirling the pan occasionally and brushing down the sides with a damp pastry brush, until you have a light golden caramel.

Recipe continued overleaf . . .

Carefully pour the caramel onto the prepared pan, swirling and tilting the pan to spread the caramel. Sprinkle with salt, and quickly scatter on the rose petals.

Cool in the fridge until hard, then break into shards. This can be prepared up to a day ahead and kept in an airtight container.

Once the pavlova is cool, decorate with the rose-infused cream, berries, pistachios, pomegranate seeds and caramel and rose shards.

Tip When making pavlova, always start with a hot 325°F (160°C) oven and then turn the temperature right down to 200–225°F (100–110°C) as soon as you have placed it in the oven. This will produce a white pavlova. Any higher and your pavlova will color to a pale golden.

If you don't have rose petals, just sprinkle the sea salt flakes on the shards before they set, and you will have salted caramel shards instead.

Spiced banoffee tarte tatin

Serves 6–8

4 tbsp (60 g) butter, chopped
¾ cup (150 g) sugar
1 cinnamon stick
4 large bananas, peeled and cut lengthways
zest of 1 orange
14 oz (400 g) store-bought puff pastry
mascarpone, crème fraîche or ice cream, to serve

This dessert reminds me of my childhood in Malawi when Mom would whip up caramelized bananas for us to have with ice cream. She would simply chop up bananas, add butter and sugar and fry them in a pan until oozy and caramelized. These flavors are just like that.

Preheat the oven to 350°F (180°C). I like to use an ovensafe skillet for this dish.

Melt the butter in your skillet over low heat, add the sugar and keep stirring until the sugar has dissolved and the mixture has caramelized and is a lovely golden color. You do need to watch it carefully—if it burns you will have to start over. Also, be extra careful as the mixture is very hot.

Add the cinnamon and place the bananas on top of the mixture—putting some facing down and some up. Remove from heat and grate the orange zest on top.

Dust a clean work surface with a little flour and roll out your pastry to about ½ in (1 cm) thick and slightly bigger than your pan. Lift the pastry and lay it over the bananas, making sure you tuck the edges in really carefully. Prick the top of the pastry a couple of times with a fork.

Bake for 25–30 minutes or until golden and puffy. You must turn out your tarte tatin as soon as it comes out of the oven. Wearing oven mits, place a large plate over the top of the skillet and quickly (and carefully) flip the skillet and plate upside down—it will be very hot so you may need an extra pair of hands. Place the plate on your work surface and carefully remove the skillet.

Serve the tarte tatin warm with mascarpone, crème fraîche or ice cream.

MENU

Alfresco indulgence

DRINK
Hibiscus &
star anise mocktail

178

APPETIZER
Zucchini &
goat cheese rosettes

144

MAIN
Baked beet & maple-glazed
side of salmon

118

SIDE
Chile & Parmesan
smashed potatoes

110

DESSERT
Pavlova crown with
caramel & rose shards

218

MENU

Inspired Indian soiree

DRINK
Mango & cardamom lassi

44

APPETIZER
Spinach fritters

155

MAIN
Lamb biryani with all the layers & crunchy filo rosettes

123

SIDE
Middle Eastern salad with pomegranate dressing

78

DESSERT
Carrot halva spring rolls

188

MENU
Festive feast

DRINK
Ginger & lime sharbat
175

APPETIZER
Spicy shrimp with puri & yogurt
164

MAIN
Slow-cooked leg of lamb on pomegranate & rose rice
133

SIDE
Harissa spice-crusted paneer & mango salad
96

DESSERT
Gulab jamun
216

MENU
Lavish Eastern banquet

DRINK
Rose, apricot & honey iced tea
47

APPETIZER
Potato bhajias with cilantro chutney
152

MAIN
Lamb parsi in spicy gravy with lemon rice
138

SIDE
Stuffed naan with turmeric apple achaar
98

DESSERT
Rose, raspberry & pistachio cream rolls
200

Extras

Plain naan
Makes 6–8 naan

3 cups (360 g) all-purpose flour
1½ tsp sugar
½ tsp salt
1 tsp baking powder
½ tsp baking soda
¼ cup (60 ml) milk
⅓ cup (80 g) plain yogurt
1 tbsp melted butter,
  plus extra for brushing
¾ cup (180 ml) warm water

Toppings (optional)
poppy seeds, cumin seeds,
  chile flakes
chopped fresh cilantro or mint

Sift the flour into a bowl, then add the sugar, salt, baking powder and baking soda and mix to combine. Make a well in the center. Add milk, yogurt, butter and water, mixing to a soft, pliable dough. On a floured work surface, knead for 5–7 minutes until smooth. Divide the dough into 6–8 portions. Roll out into oblong naan shapes 6–7 in (15–17 cm) long.

Heat a nonstick frying pan over medium–high heat. Cook each naan on one side and then place on a baking sheet and brush the uncooked side with melted butter. Add any toppings you desire. Repeat this process with the remaining naan.

Put the naan under the oven broiler until browned and blistered.

Paratha
Makes 8–10

3 cups (360 g) all-purpose or
  chapati flour, plus for dusting
½ tsp salt (optional)
1 tbsp melted ghee or butter,
  plus extra for cooking
1 cup (240 ml) warm water

Filling options
cumin seeds and ground coriander
dukkha and chile flakes
3–4 small boiled and mashed
  potatoes, mixed with salt,
  chile powder, lemon juice and
  chopped cilantro or spinach

Sift the flour and salt (if using) into a bowl. Make a well in the center, add the ghee, then water, a little at a time, and mix to a soft, pliable dough. On a floured work surface, knead for 8–10 minutes then place in a bowl and cover with a damp cloth. Set aside for 20 minutes.

Divide the dough into 8–10 portions. Roll each portion out into a 6–7 in (15–17 cm) circle. Brush the surface of the dough with ghee. Sprinkle over one of the spice mixes or add a thin layer of potato filling (not much or the mixture will leak out). Roll the dough into a tight log. Once rolled, coil into a tight disc, flatten with your palm and roll into a 6–7 in (15–17 cm) circle, dusting with flour as you go.

Heat a nonstick frying pan or griddle over medium–high heat, add melted ghee, and cook a paratha for about 10 seconds. Flip it over with a spatula and drizzle more melted ghee around the edges, tipping the pan so it is evenly distributed. Flip it again, and cook until it's golden and crisp. Set aside, covered with foil or in a warm oven, until you have cooked them all.

Roti
Makes 10–12

3 cups (360 g) all-purpose or
  chapati flour, plus for dusting
salt (optional)
2 tbsp melted ghee or butter
1 cup (240 ml) warm water

Sift the flour and salt (if using) into a bowl. Make a well in the center, add 1 tablespoon of the ghee then the water, a little at a time, mixing to a soft, pliable dough. On a floured work surface, knead for 8–10 minutes then place in a bowl and cover with a damp cloth. Set aside for 20 minutes.

Divide the dough into 10–12 equal portions. Flatten each into a disc with your hands. Smear with a little melted ghee and sprinkle with flour. Pinch the edges together to make a parcel and then roll into a ball, placing it under a damp cloth, until you have done them all.

On your floured surface, roll out each ball into a 6 in (15 cm) circle, turning the dough 90 degrees to get an even shape. You can dust with more flour while rolling, but remember to remove any excess flour at the end by placing the roti in the palm of your hand and gently slapping it from one hand to the other.

Heat a nonstick frying pan or a flat grill pan over medium–high heat. Place the roti in the hot pan for 10 seconds or until bubbles form on the underside, flip the roti and press down using a spatula as you cook the other side to make it puff up. Flip once more, pressing down again. Once cooked (after about 30 seconds), smear the roti with more melted ghee and stack on a plate. Cover with a tea towel until you have cooked them all.

Green chile & cilantro paste
Makes ½ cup (120 ml)

large bunch of fresh cilantro, stalks removed
6–8 green chiles, chopped

Blend the ingredients together with a hand blender or using a mortar and pestle.
Initially, use only ½–1 teaspoon of paste in recipes until you establish the strength of heat you like. Keeps for up to a week in the fridge or freeze for up to 3 months in ice cube trays.

Tomato chutney
Makes 1–1¼ cups (240–300 ml)

bunch of fresh cilantro, stalks removed
1 large tomato
1–3 green chiles, to taste
juice of ½ lemon
1 tsp salt
2 tbsp ketchup
1–2 tsp chile powder
½ tsp brown sugar

Place all the ingredients in a bowl and blend into a thick sauce with a hand blender. Season to taste. Store for 3–4 days in the fridge.

Tamarind chutney
Makes ¾–1 cup (180–240 ml)

2 tsp tamarind pulp or purée
3–4 tsp brown sugar
¼ tsp salt
¼ tsp ground black pepper
1 tsp cumin seeds, lightly toasted
6–8 tbsp water

Bring all the ingredients to a boil in a heavy-based pot. Simmer for a few minutes, until you have a syrupy liquid. If it gets too thick, add boiling water.
Cool and bottle in a jar. Store for up to a week in the fridge.

Cucumber raita
Makes 1–2 cups (240–480 ml)

1¾ cups (400 g) plain Greek-style yogurt
½ cup (65 g) diced cucumber
1 tbsp chopped fresh cilantro
½ tbsp chopped fresh mint
salt and ground black pepper
sprinkle of chile powder

Mix all of the ingredients together in a bowl.

Mango raita
Makes 2 cups (480 ml)

2 mangoes, peeled and finely diced
1¾ cups (400 g) plain yogurt
1 tbsp unsweetened shredded coconut
salt and ground black pepper
1 tsp sugar
¼ cup (16 g) chopped fresh cilantro leaves
1 tsp oil
¼ tsp mustard seeds
¼ tsp chile flakes

Mix the mango, yogurt, coconut, salt, pepper and sugar in a small bowl. Add the cilantro. Heat the oil in a pan, add mustard seeds and chile flakes, and heat until the seeds start popping. Cool, then pour over the raita. Best eaten on the day, or keep in the fridge for one more day.

Tomato & onion kachumber
Makes ¾–1 cup (180–240 ml)

1 large tomato, diced
1 onion, diced or 1 scallion, sliced
½ tsp chile powder
¼ tsp salt
dash of white vinegar

Mix all ingredients together in a bowl. Serve as an accompaniment to curry and rice dishes. Best eaten on the day.

With thanks

Writing a cookbook is no mean feat. Doing it while juggling family life and two jobs is not for the faint hearted. My family and friends call me "wonder woman," and often say, "How do you do it all?" I can honestly say I am not doing this alone; I have the never-ending love and support of my family and some key people who have helped me in this journey.

Graham, you are the most kind-hearted, loving and supportive partner, always encouraging me and helping me achieve all my dreams while putting yours on hold and making sure a hot cup of tea is never far away. To my beautiful children, Adam and Zara, I started this writing journey 12 years ago to leave a legacy for you both. A history of where I came from and the food I grew up with, and how sharing the recipes and feeding the people I love gave me the most pleasure. Thank you for being a part of this journey, thank you for indulging my requests to be photographed for this book. It is a treasure of memories that you will both cherish forever.

Thank you to my ISHK family all around the world (Ismail, Singer, Halimi and Kemih). I love how we are now such a multi-cultural family. Gatherings are full of food inspired by our adopted cultures. This was one of the inspirations for this book. Thank you for always being there for me. Thank you to the amazing women in my life. I love you all. Anjum, Farha and Nishat, my gorgeous sisters, thank you for your recipes that I have used in this book. Thank you, Mom, for showing me that cooking for others is pure love and joy.

To Dad, thank you for being you, it can't be easy for you to be on the other side of the world; I know it's not easy for me. Know that I love you and Mom always and forever.

Lottie Hedley, you are an incredible person, a talented photographer, calm and collected, a joy to work with. You became part of our family. Always thoughtful and generous with your never-ending supply of dahlias. We shared some tears and hugs, and I knew from the moment I saw your photography and how you worked with people that you were the perfect choice.

A big thank you to the fabulous Bateman team. Louise and Paul, for always believing in me and championing me, thank you for your enthusiasm, wisdom and support. And thank you Louise, for letting me use your beautiful table and bentwood chairs, they were perfect for my vision for this book. Sarah, you are the editor extraordinaire, your grace and patience is greatly appreciated. Hope, thank you for helping on shoot days and giving Miss Holly the cavoodle lots of cuddles. Lise, you are the best publicist, you have always promoted my books in the best possible way, everywhere!

Kate Barraclough, thank you for an amazing job on the design of this book, you have truly brought my vision to life. And Andrea Coppock, thank you for editing my words to make them flow and read so beautifully.

Thank you, Kate Arbuthnot. I have admired your work over the years, and it was fabulous to finally work with you. Your villa in Matakana was the perfect backdrop for this dream book of mine. We thoroughly enjoyed our week there. Thank you for the fabulous styling of the four menu tables and for the cover shot.

Macy, my deepest thanks for your help in the kitchen while we whizzed through all the recipe making on shoot days. Your calm and organized presence made all the difference on those crazy, hectic days.

Dave and Ruth (The Tea Thief), I fell in love with your tabletop when I met you at the Christmas markets. Thank you so much for letting me use it as a prop when photographing for my book.

Vicki (Frolic Ceramics), thank you so much for loaning me your beautiful hand-crafted ceramics, they were perfect for the modern and vintage look I was going for.

Thank you to the Curious Croppers, Anthony and Angela, for the exquisite heirloom tomatoes.

A heartfelt thanks to Al Brown and Lynda Hallinan for their generous words and taking the time to endorse my book. I am truly humbled.

Finally, thank you from the bottom of my heart to my dear readers and supporters, in person and online. It is an absolute privilege for me to share my recipes and stories with you. There is a reason I do this. It is to share my love of cooking and writing, so you can be inspired to cook my recipes for your loved ones, to gather around the table, sharing food and making memories.

Immense gratitude always,
Ashia

Index

A

achaar
  Stuffed naan with turmeric apple achaar 98
almond
  Galette des rois 196
  Orange & rose almond cake 210
Anj's chicken sharwama in naan with pickled onions 77
apple
  Stuffed naan with turmeric apple achaar 98
apricot
  Chicken tagine with apricots served with couscous 130
  Rose, apricot & honey iced tea 47

B

baked Alaska
  Mango & cardamom semifreddo with baked Alaska 199
Baked beet & maple-glazed side of salmon 118
Baklava cheesecake with orange blossom syrup 202
banana
  Spiced banoffee tarte tatin 223
beef
  Koftas with marinated feta in thyme & chile oil 57
beet
  Baked beet & maple-glazed side of salmon 118
bhajia
  Potato bhajias with cilantro chutney 152
bhel 95
biryani
  Lamb biryani with all the layers & crunchy filo rosettes 123
blueberry
  Cinnamon & cardamom breakfast doughnuts with blueberry compote 31
borek
  Mediterranean spiced lamb borek 128
bread
  Cinnamon & cardamom breakfast doughnuts with blueberry compote 31
  Cumin puri with mango chutney 169
  Herby ciabatta with ricotta & cherries 28
  Kesra bread with whipped feta & sumac-roasted chickpeas 170
  Paratha 241
  Plain naan 241
  Roti 241
  Spiced hot-smoked salmon served with homemade crackers 156
  Stuffed naan with turmeric apple achaar 98

C

cake
  Baklava cheesecake with orange blossom syrup 202
  Orange & rose almond cake 210
  Peach meringue cake 193
  Strawberry Charlotte cake 186
caramel
  Pavlova crown with caramel & rose shards 218
cardamom
  Cinnamon & cardamom breakfast doughnuts with blueberry compote 31
  Mango & cardamom semifreddo with baked Alaska 199
carrot
  Carrot halva spring roll 188
cassava
  Cassava & vegetable stew 104
  Cassava fries with chile & lime 172
cheesecake
  Baklava cheesecake with orange blossom syrup 202
cherry
  Herby ciabatta with ricotta & cherries 28
chicken
  Anj's chicken sharwama in naan with pickled onions 77
  Chicken pakoras in a curry leaf batter 166
  Chicken tagine with apricots served with couscous 130
  North African chicken bastilla pie 141
  Whole roast chicken with spicy gravy & vegetable pilau rice 120
chickpeas
  Kesra bread with whipped feta & sumac-roasted chickpeas 170
chile
  Cassava fries with chile & lime 172
  Chile & Parmesan smashed potatoes 110
  Fried harissa-spiced eggplants with a sizzling chile yogurt 89
  Koftas with marinated feta in thyme & chile oil 57
  Parmesan-crumbed paneer with chile & mayo 150
  Peach, honey, goat cheese & chile salad 106
  Spice-roasted vegetables with haloumi & a cilantro-chile dressing 84
  Tuna & green chile croquettes 163
chutney
  cilantro chutney 152
  cilantro garlic chutney 26
  mango chutney 60
  Tamarind chutney 242
  Tomato chutney 242
cilantro
  cilantro chutney 152
  cilantro garlic chutney 26
  Green chile & cilantro paste 242
  Spice-roasted vegetables with haloumi & a cilantro-chile dressing 84
cinnamon
  Cinnamon & cardamom breakfast doughnuts with blueberry compote 31
  Cinnamon plum clafoutis 215

clafoutis
  Cinnamon plum clafoutis 215
compote
  blueberry compote 31
corn
  Masala corn on the cob 52
  Zucchini & corn sliders with mango chutney 60
couscous
  Chicken tagine with apricots served with couscous 130
cracker *see* bread
crème brûlée
  Rhubarb & star anise crème brûlée 208
croquettes
  Tuna & green chile croquettes 163
Cucumber raita 242
Cumin puri with mango chutney 169
curry
  Egg curry with paratha 90
  Kitchari with pea & green bean curry 112
  Lamb biryani with all the layers & crunchy filo rosettes 123
  Lamb parsi in spicy gravy with lemon rice 138
  Machi fry with fried onions & naan 136
  Spicy kidney beans with rice 109
curry leaf
  Chicken pakoras in a curry leaf batter 166
  Fried curry leaves & crumbed olives 181
  Roast sweet potato with curry leaf & mustard seed yogurt 92

D

dessert
  Cinnamon plum clafoutis 215
  Gulab jamun 216
  Halva with scarlet poached pears 207
  Mango & cardamom semifreddo with baked Alaska 199
  Rhubarb & star anise crème brûlée 208
doughnut
  Cinnamon & cardamom breakfast doughnuts with blueberry compote 31
dressing
  cilantro & chile dressing 84, 96
  maple dressing 32
  pomegranate dressing 78
drink
  Ginger & lime sharbat 175
  Hibiscus & star anise mocktail 178
  Raspberry & rose water limeade 176
  Rose, apricot & honey iced tea 47
  Sweet & salty lassis 44

E

Egg curry with paratha 90
eggplant
  Fried harissa-spiced eggplants with a sizzling chile yogurt 89
  Middle Eastern salad with pomegranate dressing 78
  Smoked whole baby eggplants coated in spicy egg 42
empanada
  Spiced pumpkin & sweet potato empanadas 67

F

feta
  Kesra bread with whipped feta & sumac-roasted chickpeas 170
  Koftas with marinated feta in thyme & chile oil 57
  Spinach, feta & pine nut tart 86
  Watermelon, feta & maple salad 32
fish
  Machi fry with fried onions & naan 136
  Tuna & green chile croquettes 163
Fried curry leaves & crumbed olives 181
Fried harissa-spiced eggplants with a sizzling chile yogurt 89
fritter
  Spinach fritters 155

G

Galette des rois 196
Ginger & lime sharbat 175
goat cheese
  Peach, honey, goat cheese & chile salad 106
  Tomato & goat cheese tart 62
  Zucchini & goat cheese rosettes 144
green bean
  Kitchari with pea & green bean curry 112
Green chile & cilantro paste 242
Gulab jamun 216
Gunpowder masala crispy choux potatoes 103

H

haloumi
  Spice-roasted vegetables with haloumi & a cilantro-chile dressing 84
halva
  Carrot halva spring roll 188
  Halva with scarlet poached pears 207
Harissa spice-crusted paneer & mango salad 96
Herby ciabatta with ricotta & cherries 28
Hibiscus & star anise mocktail 178
Hot-smoked salmon quiche 68

K

kachumber
  Tomato & onion kachumber 242
Kathi rolls with pickled onion & lamb kebab 20
kebab
  Kathi rolls with pickled onion & lamb kebab 20
Kesra bread with whipped feta &

sumac-roasted chickpeas 170
kidney beans
  Spicy kidney beans with rice 109
Kitchari with pea & green bean curry 112
Koftas with marinated feta in thyme & chile oil 57
Kokum batata with bhel 95

L

labneh 72
  Mixed heirloom tomato & labneh salad 72
lamb
  Kathi rolls with pickled onion & lamb kebab 20
  Lamb biryani with all the layers & crunchy filo rosettes 123
  Lamb parsi in spicy gravy with lemon rice 138
  Mediterranean spiced lamb borek 128
  Slow-cooked leg of lamb on pomegranate & rose rice 133
  Spiced lamb shakshuka 36
  Spicy ground lamb & pea hand pies with chutney 54
lassi
  Sweet & salty lassis 44
lemon
  Lamb parsi in spicy gravy with lemon rice 138
lime
  Cassava fries with chile & lime 172
  Ginger & lime sharbat 175
limeade
  Raspberry & rose water limeade 176

M

Machi fry with fried onions & naan 136
mango
  Harissa spice-crusted paneer & mango salad 96
  Mango & cardamom semifreddo with baked Alaska 199
  mango chutney 60
Mango raita 242
maple dressing 32
masala
  Gunpowder masala crispy choux potatoes 103
  Masala corn on the cob 52
mayonnaise
  Parmesan-crumbed paneer with chile & mayo 150
Mediterranean spiced lamb borek 128
meringue
  Mango & cardamom semifreddo with baked Alaska 199
  Pavlova crown with caramel & rose shards 218
  Peach meringue cake 193
Middle Eastern salad with pomegranate dressing 78
Mixed heirloom tomato & labneh salad 72
mustard seed
  Roast sweet potato with curry leaf & mustard seed yogurt 92

N

naan *see* bread
North African chicken bastilla pie 141

O

olive
  Fried curry leaves & crumbed olives 181
onion
  Machi fry with fried onions & naan 136
  pickled onion 20
  Tomato & onion kachumber 242
orange
  Baklava cheesecake with orange blossom syrup 202
  Orange & rose almond cake 210

P

pakora
  Chicken pakoras in a curry leaf batter 166
pancake
  Strawberry cheesecake pancakes 38
paneer
  Harissa spice-crusted paneer & mango salad 96
  Parmesan-crumbed paneer with chile & mayo 150
Pani puri with potato filling & tamarind & cilantro chutney 160
Paratha 241
Parmesan
  Chile & Parmesan smashed potatoes 110
  Parmesan-crumbed paneer with chile & mayo 150
paste
  Green chile & cilantro paste 242
pastry
  Carrot halva spring roll 188
  Zucchini & goat cheese rosettes 144
  Cumin puri with mango chutney 169
  Galette des rois 196
  Gunpowder masala crispy choux potatoes 103
  Hot-smoked salmon quiche 68
  Lamb biryani with all the layers & crunchy filo rosettes 123
  Mediterranean spiced lamb borek 128
  Pani puri with potato filling & tamarind & cilantro chutney 160
  Rose & Berry Paris–Brest 194
  Rose, raspberry & pistachio cream rolls 200
  Spiced banoffee tarte tatin 223
  Spiced pumpkin & sweet potato empanadas 67
  Spicy ground lamb & pea hand pies with chutney 54
  Spicy shrimp with puri & yogurt 164
  Spinach, feta & pine nut tart 86
  Tomato & goat cheese tart 62
  Vegetarian samosa chaat 25

Pav bhaji 41
Pavlova crown with caramel & rose shards 218
pea
  Kitchari with pea & green bean curry 112
  Spicy ground lamb & pea hand pies with chutney 54
peach
  Peach, honey, goat cheese & chile salad 106
  Peach meringue cake 193
pear
  Halva with scarlet poached pears 207
pepper
  Middle Eastern salad with pomegranate dressing 78
pickled onion 20
pie
  North African chicken bastilla pie 141
  Spicy ground lamb & pea hand pies with chutney 54
pine nut
  Spinach, feta & pine nut tart 86
pistachio
  Rose, raspberry & pistachio cream rolls 200
Plain naan 241
plum
  Cinnamon plum clafoutis 215
pomegranate
  pomegranate dressing 78
  Slow-cooked leg of lamb on pomegranate & rose rice 133
potato
  Chile & Parmesan smashed potatoes 110
  Gunpowder masala crispy choux potatoes 103
  Kokum batata with bhel 95
  Pani puri with potato filling & tamarind & cilantro chutney 160
  Pav bhaji 41
  Potato bhajias with cilantro chutney 152
  Vegetarian samosa chaat 25
pumpkin
  Spiced pumpkin & sweet potato empanadas 67
puri *see* pastry

Q
quiche
  Hot-smoked salmon quiche 68

R
raita
  Cucumber raita 242
  Mango raita 242
raspberry
  Raspberry & rose water limeade 176
  Rose & Berry Paris–Brest 194
  Rose, raspberry & pistachio cream rolls 200
Rhubarb & star anise crème brûlée 208
rice
  Kitchari with pea & green bean curry 112
  Lamb biryani with all the layers & crunchy filo rosettes 123
  Lamb parsi in spicy gravy with lemon rice 138
  Slow-cooked leg of lamb on pomegranate & rose rice 133
  Whole roast chicken with spicy gravy & vegetable pilau rice 120
ricotta
  Herby ciabatta with ricotta & cherries 28
Roast sweet potato with curry leaf & mustard seed yogurt 92
rose
  Orange & rose almond cake 210
  Pavlova crown with caramel & rose shards 218
  Raspberry & rose water limeade 176
  Rose & Berry Paris–Brest 194
  Rose, apricot & honey iced tea 47
  Rose, raspberry & pistachio cream rolls 200
  Slow-cooked leg of lamb on pomegranate & rose rice 133
  sugared rose petals 194
Roti 241

S
saffron rice 123
salad
  Harissa spice-crusted paneer & mango salad 96
  Middle Eastern salad with pomegranate dressing 78
  Mixed heirloom tomato & labneh salad 72
  Peach, honey, goat cheese & chile salad 106
  Watermelon, feta & maple salad 32
salmon
  Baked beet & maple-glazed side of salmon 118
  Hot-smoked salmon quiche 68
  Spiced hot-smoked salmon served with homemade crackers 156
samosa
  Vegetarian samosa chaat 25
sauce
  tamarind sauce 95
  yogurt curry sauce 112
semifreddo
  Mango & cardamom semifreddo with baked Alaska 199
shakshuka
  Spiced lamb shakshuka 36
sharbat
  Ginger & lime sharbat 175
sharwama
  Anj's chicken sharwama in naan with pickled onions 77
shrimp
  Spicy shrimp with puri & yogurt 164
sliders
  Zucchini & corn sliders with mango chutney 60
Slow-cooked leg of lamb on pomegranate & rose rice 133
Smoked whole baby eggplants coated in spicy egg 42
Spice-roasted vegetables with

haloumi & a cilantro-chile
    dressing 84
Spiced banoffee tarte tatin 223
Spiced hot-smoked salmon served
    with homemade crackers 156
Spiced lamb shakshuka 36
Spiced pumpkin & sweet potato
    empanadas 67
Spicy kidney beans with rice 109
Spicy ground lamb & pea hand pies
    with chutney 54
Spicy shrimp with puri
    & yogurt 164
spinach
    Spinach, feta & pine nut tart 86
    Spinach fritters 155
spring roll
    Carrot halva spring roll 188
star anise
    Hibiscus & star anise mocktail 178
    Rhubarb & star anise
        crème brûlée 208
strawberry
    Strawberry Charlotte cake 186
    Strawberry cheesecake
        pancakes 38
Stuffed naan with turmeric apple
    achaar 98
sugared rose petals 194
sumac
    Kesra bread with whipped feta &
        sumac-roasted chickpeas 170
sweet potato
    Roast sweet potato with curry leaf &
        mustard seed yogurt 92
    Spiced pumpkin & sweet potato
        empanadas 67
Sweet & salty lassis 44
sweetcorn see corn

T

tagine
    Chicken tagine with apricots served
        with couscous 130
tamarind
    Kokum batata with bhel 95
    Tamarind chutney 242
tart
    Spinach, feta & pine nut tart 86
    Tomato & goat cheese tart 62
tea see drinks
tomato
    Middle Eastern salad with
        pomegranate dressing 78
    Mixed heirloom tomato &
        labneh salad 72
    Tomato & goat cheese tart 62
    Tomato & onion kachumber 242
    Tomato chutney 242
Tuna & green chile croquettes 163
turmeric
    Stuffed naan with turmeric apple
        achaar 98

V

Vegetarian samosa chaat 25

W

Watermelon, feta & maple salad
    32
Whole roast chicken with
    spicy gravy & vegetable
    pilau rice 120

Y

yogurt
    Cucumber raita 242
    Fried harissa-spiced eggplants with
        a sizzling chile yogurt 89
    Mango raita 242
    mustard seed yogurt 92
    Roast sweet potato with curry leaf &
        mustard seed yogurt 92
    Spicy shrimp with puri &
        yogurt 164
    yogurt curry sauce 112

Z

zucchini
    Zucchini & corn sliders with mango
        chutney 60
    Zucchini & goat cheese
        rosettes 144

Published in 2025 by

Interlink Books
An imprint of Interlink Publishing Group, Inc.
46 Crosby Street
Northampton, Massachusetts 01060
www.interlinkbooks.com

Published in New Zealand by David Bateman Ltd.
Unit 2/5 Workspace Drive, Hobsonville,
Auckland 0618, New Zealand

Text © Ashia Ismail-Singer, 2024
Photography © Lottie Hedley, 2024
Typographical design © David Bateman Ltd, 2024

All rights reserved. No part of this publication may be reproduced, stored in a retrieval system or transmitted in any form or by any means, electronic, mechanical, photocopying, recording, or otherwise, without the prior written permission of the publisher.

Library-of-Congress Data available
ISBN: 978-1-62371-629-5

American edition editor: Leyla Moushabeck
American edition proofreader: Jane Bugaeva
Book design: Kate Barraclough
Cover design: Harrison Williams
Styling and props: Ashia Ismail-Singer & Lottie Hedley
Styling for menu shots: Kate Arbuthnot
Family photographs on page 11 supplied by Ashia Ismail-Singer

Printed and bound in Korea

MIX
Paper | Supporting
responsible forestry
FSC® C023083